AFTER THE CAR

D1334027

AFTER THE CAR

KINGSLEY DENNIS
AND JOHN URRY

polity

The right of Kingsley Dennis and John Urry to be identified as Authors of this Work has been asserted in accordance with the UK Copyright, Designs and Patents Act 1988.

First published in 2009 by Polity Press
Reprinted 2009 (twice)

Polity Press
65 Bridge Street
Cambridge CB2 1UR, UK.

Polity Press
350 Main Street
Malden, MA 02148, USA.

ISBN-13: 978-0-7456-4421-9
ISBN-13: 978-0-7456-4422-6 (pb)

A catalogue record for this book is available from the British Library.

Typeset in 10.75 on 14 pt in Adobe Sabon
by Servis Filmsetting Ltd, Stockport, Cheshire
Printed and bound by MPG Books Group, UK

The publisher has used its best endeavours to ensure that the URLs for external websites referred to in this book are correct and active at the time of going to press. However, the publisher has no responsibility for the websites and can make no guarantee that a site will remain live or that the content is or will remain appropriate.

Every effort has been made to trace all copyright holders, but if any have been inadvertently overlooked the publisher will be pleased to include any necessary credits in any subsequent reprint or edition.

For further information on Polity, visit our website: www.politybooks.com

CONTENTS

PREFACE

We are very grateful to the following colleagues, mostly at Lancaster, with whom we have discussed these various post-car futures: Monika Büscher, Noel Cass, Tim Dant, Sergio Fava, Drew Hemment, Michael Hulme, Bob Jessop, John Law, Will Medd, Tom Roberts, Daniela Sangiorgi, Andrew Sayer, Dan Shapiro, Mimi Sheller, Elizabeth Shove, Bron Szerszynski, David Tyfield, Sylvia Walby, Laura Watts, James Wilsdon and Brian Wynne. John Urry is grateful for his involvement in the DTi Foresight discussions on Intelligent Information Systems in 2005–6, as well as recent research funding from the Department for Transport, ESRC and the EPSRC.

We also wish to acknowledge the research opportunities afforded to us by the Centre for Mobilities Research (CeMoRe) at Lancaster. This Centre has stimulated much debate on the issues presented in this book. We are especially grateful to Pennie Drinkall for all her hard work for CeMoRe. Many similar issues to those discussed in this book are debated on CeMoRe's blog at www.new-mobilities.co.uk.

Lancaster, September 2008

1

CHANGING CLIMATES

ENDING THE CAR

This book would seem to have an implausible title. How on earth can we imagine that there could be an end to the car, that we can envisage a system that is 'after the car'? In some ways the car and its associated activities and technologies is the most powerful product or system there has been over the last century or so. Some have described the twentieth century as the century of the car.[1] Over a billion cars have been manufactured and over 650 million currently roam the world's roads and streets. It is predicted that, if nothing changes, within a couple of decades there will be 1 billion cars worldwide, especially as China fully moves from a bike society to a car society.

Moreover, we do not think that we can turn the clock back and that the individual flexibility, comfort and convenience that the car provides is going to disappear. It is unlikely that everyone in the future will be travelling on foot and by bike, and especially not by public bus and train. So what could we be saying here if we claim that the end might be in sight for the extraordinary car system that has so far 'driven' out all its many competitors?

When we talk of 'after the car,' we are suggesting that the car as a complete system may be surpassed. The current car system involves a number of key features: cars are made of steel, mostly powered by petrol (or 'gasoline' in the US), each can seat four people, they are personally owned, and each is driven independently of others, although certain rules do need to be followed and enforced.

Our argument in this book is that some very powerful forces around the world are undermining this car system and will usher in a new system at some point in this century. The car system is based upon nineteenth-century technologies, of steel bodies and internal combustion engines, incidentally showing how old technologies can remarkably endure. We believe that this mass system of individualized, flexible mobility will be 'redesigned' and 're-engineered' before the end of this century. This book argues that a new system is coming into being. It is a bit like the period around 1900 when the current car system was being formed: it was emergent, although no one at the time could imagine exactly what it was going to be like.

So, similarly, we hold that a wide array of changes are occurring across the world – changes of technology, policy, economy and society, which are all elements of this new system that is as yet nowhere actually in place. And it will be through the dynamic interdependence of the various parts that will bring into being this new system that is 'after the car'. This book thus explores a new 'socio-technical' system that we believe is in the making.

In this chapter, we consider various dynamic changes 'in the climate' within which travel and transportation are being organized and implemented in the twenty-first century. If these changes converge and impact upon each other, they may generate shifts beyond the car that would involve a low carbon economy and society. We begin with an analysis of climate *per se*. This is followed by an analysis of the apparent peaking of the supply of oil around the world. We then examine some of the changes in the nature of the virtual world, of computers, software and security, before considering the growth of population and especially of mega-cities in the contemporary world.

This chapter thus examines the changing climates of change surrounding transport and energy and how they may be engendering a new system that will be 'after the car' and hence could entail a lower carbon future society, albeit one which is by no means a simply positive future. We will examine various futures and see that all possess a dark side due to the constrained choices that the high carbon twentieth century provided as a legacy going into the new century.

CLIMATE CHANGE

We begin by paying especial attention to global climate change, reflected in 2006 in Al Gore's surprising PowerPoint hit *An Inconvenient Truth* and his subsequent Nobel prize.[2] This film brought home to the world the fact that global temperatures have risen over the past century (by at least 0.74°C) and this seems to be the consequence of higher levels of greenhouse gases in the earth's atmosphere. Even the Pentagon announced that climate change will result in a global catastrophe costing millions of lives in wars and natural disasters. And they state that the threat to global stability far eclipses that of terrorism.[3]

Greenhouse gases trap the sun's rays. As a result of this 'greenhouse' effect the earth warms. Such greenhouse gas

levels and world temperatures will apparently increase significantly over the next few decades. Such warming will
change patterns of temperatures worldwide and result in
a greatly increased frequency of extreme weather events.[4]
Such climate change resulting from increasing greenhouse
gas emissions constitutes the world's major threat to human
life and social organization.

The scientific evidence for climate change is now
less uncertain compared with the time when the first
Intergovernmental Panel on Climate Change (IPCC) Report
appeared in 1990. The 2007 Report makes a number of separate claims. First, in the 2007 Report the IPCC declared
that the warming of the world's climate is now 'unequivocal'.
This claim is based upon extensive observations of increases
in global average air and ocean temperatures, the widespread
melting of snow and ice, and rising global average sea levels.

Second, the 2007 Report shows that carbon dioxide is the
most important of the human-produced or anthropogenic
greenhouse gases. Its concentration levels exceed by far the
natural range identified over the past 650,000 years. Its high
and rising levels must thus stem, it is concluded, from 'non-
natural' causes.

Third, there is very high confidence amongst the thousands of scientists involved in the IPCC that such global
warming is the effect of human activities that, in many different ways, have resulted in dramatically raised levels of
carbon emissions.

And fourth, there are many different physical consequences of global warming: increase in arctic temperatures,
reduced size of icebergs, melting of ice-caps and glaciers,
reduced permafrost, changes in rainfall patterns, new wind
formations, droughts, heat waves, tropical cyclones and other
extreme weather events.[5] The IPCC projects increased risks
of flooding for tens of millions of people due to storms and

sea-level rises, especially in the poor south of the globe, in particular Bangladesh. In addition to increased fresh water scarcity, there may also be sudden rises in new vector-borne diseases (malaria, dengue fever) and water-borne disease (cholera). The World Health Organization calculated as early as 2000 that over 150,000 deaths are caused each year by climate change, such changes being global, cross-generational and highly unequal around the world.

Moreover, these IPCC Reports are based on reaching scientific and political consensus. They tend to the more cautious interpretation of the scientific evidence and do not factor in all the feedback effects that are occurring and may develop over the next few decades.[6] Levels of greenhouse gases and world temperatures will significantly increase over these decades, but these increases will almost certainly trigger *further* temperature increases through what are known as positive feedbacks (see chapter 3 below). Negative feedback would restore the earth's equilibrium, while positive feedbacks will move any system away from equilibrium. And according to James Lovelock 'there is no large negative feedback that would countervail temperature rise'.[7]

The most dramatic of these positive feedbacks would be the melting of Greenland's ice-cap, which would change sea and land temperatures worldwide, including the possible turning off or modification of the Gulf Stream. A series of diverse yet interconnected changes within the earth's environmental systems could create a vicious circle of accumulative disruption occurring, as Fred Pearce expresses it, 'with speed and violence'. Indeed the melting of the West Antarctic ice sheet may happen very rapidly (and may already have started). The ice-cap will disintegrate from above and from below and this non-linear change further reduces the rate at which heat gets reflected back to the sun. The historic record shows that these ice-caps have historically formed and disappeared with 'speed and violence'. If the West Antarctic ice sheet were to disintegrate, then rather than the sea level increasing by 18 to 59 cm over this century as the IPCC predicts, it could rise by many metres. As a consequence, most human settlements located close to the ocean's edge would be washed away and there would be massive population loss around the world.[8]

The recent study of ice cores shows how previous glacial and interglacial periods demonstrated very abrupt changes in the earth's temperature. Such rapid changes were the norm, not the exception. Moreover, the temperatures at the time of the last Ice Age were only 5°C colder than they are today. And in the Arctic such increases have been really marked, with feedbacks creating local warming of 3–5°C over just the past thirty years. Fred Pearce thus notes: 'The big discovery is that planet Earth does not generally engage in gradual change. It is far cruder and nastier'.[9]

With 'business as usual' and no significant reductions in the world's high carbon systems, the stock of greenhouse gases could treble by the end of the century. The Stern Review states that there is a 50 per cent risk of more than a 5°C increase in temperatures by 2100. This would transform the world's physical and human geography through a 5–20 per cent reduction in world consumption levels.[10] Even a temperature increase worldwide of 3°C is completely beyond any recent experience of temperature change and would totally transform animal, plant and human life as they have been known.

Some climate change effects are already being experienced in the world's insurance industry. Due to increased risks of flooding, the Association of British Insurers may not be able to continue to provide cover since the £800 million a year pledged by 2011 for flood defences is deemed insufficient.[11] Insurance losses worldwide have seen a sudden rise, with much evidence that extreme weather is responsible for these globally rising costs. Since the 1970s they have risen around 10 per cent annually. Science writer Tim Flannery wrote recently that 'such a rate of increase implies that by 2065 or soon thereafter, the damage bill resulting from climate change may equal the total value of everything that humanity produced in the course of a year'.[12]

According to Fred Pearce, insured losses from extreme weather in 2004 hit a record $55 billion, exceeded a year later by $70 billion.[13] And the costs associated with cleaning up after Hurricane Katrina could run to $100 billion. And the future only looks set to see trends of rising insurance claims from extreme weather. In 2001, Munich Re (the world's largest reinsurance company) estimated that by 2050 the annual global damage bill from climate change could top £250 billion, with insurance industry leaders doubting that they can absorb these claims for much longer. More generally, the UK Stern Review argues that taking no action now with regard to climate change will ultimately prove to be much more costly than the sums that are required for taking immediate action.[14]

Various macro-scale technologies have been suggested to combat climate change, such as seeding the ocean with iron filings, spraying nano-chemicals into the atmosphere, or putting sunshades in space. None, however, could be implemented on a sufficient scale to combat climate change for many decades.

There is also the danger that proponents of climate change neglect other processes producing climatic variation.[15] But as one commentator recently stated:

> It may not matter any more whether global warming is or is not a by-product of human activity, or if it just represents the dynamic disequilibrium of what we call 'nature'. But it happens to coincide with our imminent descent down the slippery slope of oil and gas depletion, so that all the

potential discontinuities of that epochal circumstance will be amplified, ramified, reinforced, and torqued by climate change.[16]

So overall consequences of such unique changes are global and, if they are not significantly reduced, they will very substantially reduce the standard of living, the capabilities of life around the world and overall population as catastrophic impacts begin, starting off in the 'poor' south. The planet will endure, but many forms of human habitation will not if business continues as usual.

And to slow down, let alone reverse, increasing carbon emissions and temperatures requires nothing more and nothing less than the reorganization of social life. The nature of 'social life' is central to the causes, the consequences and the possible 'mitigations' involved in global heating. Yet nowhere in the major analyses of climate change are there good understandings of how to bring about transformed sets of human activities. Most official reports are written by scientists for scientists and governments and are uninformed by social science. This is true even of the very significant Stern Review, which does not develop an analysis of how human practices are organized over time and space and how they might be significantly transformed. Changing human activities is mostly seen as a matter of modifying economic incentives through, for example, different tax rates.[17] And to be fair, the social sciences have engaged little with the sciences of climate change, although Ulrich Beck published his pertinent text on risk society well over twenty years ago.[18]

Around the world, there are many organizations and a few governments that are making it clear that there is a window of opportunity of maybe a couple of decades during which to intervene on a major scale to slow down global heating. James Hansen, Bush's main climate change adviser, is very clear: 'We are on the precipice of climate change tipping points beyond which there is no redemption'.[19] After that window of opportunity, the various 'human activities' that are generating increased carbon emissions will make further warming of the planet inevitable *and* probably catastrophic. This is what James Lovelock terms the 'revenge of Gaia' that is engendering 'global heating'.[20]

The approach we adopt in this book is one of analysing system developments and system changes. Climate change we see as the outcome of enormously powerful systems that are rather like a 'juggernaut' careering at full speed towards the edge of a cliff.[21] And slowing down the juggernaut even slightly requires the engendering of equally if not more powerful systems than those currently powering it towards this fast approaching abyss.

The futurologist Buckminster Fuller famously said: 'You never change anything by fighting the existing reality. To change something, build a new model that makes the existing model obsolete'.[22] Our concern here, then, is not analysing what some refer to as the gap between values (to slow down climate change) and behaviour (continuing to drive or heat one's house to high temperatures). Rather, we examine the potential of system change. Is there a new model that could develop here? Could the car system come to be replaced with a 'new model' or system?

Slowing down the juggernaut requires new systems, in this case a system that surpasses the car by providing flexibilized, comfortable and secure personal mobility that is not based on the high energy system of the existing car system. It is necessary to develop a system that is 'after the car', but which does not totally displace certain of the car's undoubted virtues. If it did, the alternative would not take over.

Reducing carbon use within transport is crucial, since it accounts for 14 per cent of total greenhouse gas emissions.

It is the second fastest growing source of such emissions and this figure is expected to double by 2050.[23] There have been huge increases in the speed of travel and in the distances that are covered. In 1800, people in the US travelled 50 metres a day – they now travel 50 kilometres a day. Today, world citizens move 23 billion kilometres; by 2050 that figure could quadruple to 106 billion if 'business' continues as usual.[24]

Central to such transport-generated emissions are those generated by car travel. In 2004, the UK transport sector was responsible for around 27 per cent of total carbon dioxide emissions, most of this coming from road traffic. This figure had risen by about 10 per cent compared with the previous decade. Further, a UK Department of Trade and Industry (DTI) forecast stated that CO_2 emissions from traffic in the UK will increase by 15 per cent from 2000 levels by 2015. It seems more and more unlikely that the UK Government will be able to meet its target to reduce domestic CO_2 emissions by 20 per cent by 2010.[25]

The US Environmental Protection Agency estimated that 60 per cent of all US carbon dioxide emissions are emitted by motor vehicles.[26] The US, with 5 per cent of the world's population, has 30 per cent of the world's cars and produces an extraordinary 45 per cent of the world's car-derived CO_2 emissions.[27] 95 per cent of transport is powered by oil and half of all oil is used in transportation, including maritime shipping and cargo vessels. The fate of the oil industry and its consequences for climate change and continued high levels of movement are absolutely crucial. As Rob Routs, Executive Director at Shell said in 2006: 'since the marriage of fossil fuels and the internal combustion engine some hundred years ago, the fortunes of our industries have been tied together'.[28] Indeed, many of the world's leading corporations in the twentieth century are either manufacturers of cars or suppliers of oil.

This book focuses upon this car system that is overwhelmingly significant for contemporary life, so significant in fact that it is often not really noticed lurking in the background. We will endeavour to see whether and to what degree one of the major systems powering the climate change juggernaut to the cliff's edge might just get replaced by an alternative low carbon system. So this is one sense of the title 'after the car' of this book. Such a new system will necessarily involve integrating personal movement with digital information flows. Each vehicle will need to be 'tracked and traced' and its movement and carbon footprint monitored on various databases. One issue we thus will have to deal with is how to design and develop a low carbon post-car system that does not become like George Orwell's *1984* with 'Big Brother' forms of surveillance.[29] Given the tendency towards new kinds of surveillance activated by most states in response to the crises of September 11th and the so-called 'war on terror', this is a major challenge for design. How to design for sustainability without simultaneously enhancing the many extensive forms of personal surveillance in the contemporary world?

But there is another way of moving to 'after the car' over the next few decades. If the reverse gear cannot be found, then global heating and the end of cheap, plentiful oil could erode the very bases of the current car system (and all similar high carbon systems). Flooding, droughts, extreme weather events, water and oil wars could result in the break-up of long-distance oil and gas supplies and more generally of communications. The systems that made possible the current car system will disappear and the end of the car will occur through a dystopic nightmare. There are visions of this in recent reports as to the future from the European Union, in the movie *The Day After Tomorrow* and in Sarah Hall's recent novel *The Carhullan Army*, where long-distance movement more or less disappears in a bleak post-oil future.[30]

So the car will end at some stage during the current century. This might occur through the emergence of a new system that is 'after the car'. This is what transport researchers Robin Hickman and David Banister term: 'a real step change in travel behaviour and emissions' that might generate a whole new wave of development.[31] This could be something like the way mobile phones appeared from 'nowhere' and replaced landline phones through an entirely new system. Or we might move to 'after the car' through a climate change collapse reinforced by declining oil supplies.

We will also show that most of the problems we are now confronted with derive from the twentieth century. In that century, an enormous number of powerful high carbon systems were set in place, locked in through various economic and social institutions.[32] And as the century unfolded, those lock-ins meant that the world was left a high carbon legacy whose consequences are only now being acknowledged. The steel-and-petroleum car is one of those locked-in legacies that need to be got rid of, but we will also show that its passing will not enable the world to leap into some utopian nirvana. Getting rid of the car system and other high carbon systems is utterly necessary but it involves costly processes. The twentieth century is reaping its revenge upon the twenty-first century and limiting the choices and opportunities that are available.

And in the new century various societies are playing carbon catch-up. The most spectacular is China, about to become the world's largest emitter of greenhouse gases and as a developing country not yet under Kyoto and needing to reduce its carbon emissions. This is undermining global initiatives at emission reduction, since increases in China's greenhouse gases annul any cuts made by the rich north. Short-term reductions in China's emissions seem unlikely, since it is the world's largest coal producer and a new burst in building coal-fuelled power stations is underway, partly in response to power cuts experienced in 2004. Significantly, though, Beijing has announced plans to generate 10 per cent of its power from renewable sources by 2010 and it does have plans to build various eco-cities, which we examine below.[33]

Paradoxically, the delivery of fresh water also depends on fossil fuels and already severe water shortages face one-third of the world's population.[34] As a further convergence of oil impacts upon the environment, whatever oil does to the water and land, it also does to the earth's atmosphere. Every gallon of petrol discharges twenty-four pounds of heat-trapping emissions, according to the Union of Concerned Scientists.[35]

And one crucial reason for potential global disaster is how systems interact with each other. There are dynamic shocks stemming from climate change and the shortages of oil and gas. Homer-Dixon notes: 'I think the kind of crisis we might see would be a result of systems that are kind of stressed to the max already . . . societies face crisis when they're hit by multiple shocks simultaneously or they're affected by multiple stresses simultaneously'.[36] Human and physical systems exist in states of dynamic tension and are especially vulnerable to dynamic instabilities. We examine in this book how various systems reverberate against each other and their impact on larger systemic changes. It is the simultaneity of converging shifts that creates significant changes. Thus, resource depletion (peak oil) and climate change may come to overload a fragile global system, creating the possibility of catastrophic failure unless those high carbon systems from the twentieth century have begun to be displaced.[37]

Human civilizations have in the past disappeared, and it may be that the current patterns of civilization could also be on earth only for a finite period of time. And the disaster of climate change is increasingly intersecting with a global energy crisis, since it seems that oil (and gas) supplies around

the world are about to start running down. We now turn
directly to this issue.

PEAK OIL

Today's global economy is deeply dependent upon, and
embedded in, abundant cheap oil. Most industrial, agricultural, commercial, domestic and consumer systems are
built around the plentiful supply of 'black gold', as oil is
often called. The peaking of oil and production decline will
strongly affect global markets, as well as the many financial
institutions that rely on stable market conditions.

The peak oil hypothesis states that the extracting of oil
reserves has a beginning, a middle and an end. And at some
point it reaches maximum output, with the peak occurring
when approximately half the potential oil has been extracted.
After this, oil becomes more difficult and expensive to extract
as each field ages past the mid-point of its life.[38] Oil production typically follows a bell-shaped curve when charted on
a graph, following the Hubbert's peak model.[39] This does
not mean oil suddenly runs out, but the supply of cheap oil
drops and prices rise, possibly dramatically. After peak oil,
the oil extraction process becomes less profitable. This ratio
is referred to as the Energy Return on Energy Investment
(EROEI).

Some predictions suggest that global peak oil occurred as
early as the late 1990s. Others estimate that global production
of conventional oil peaked either in the spring of 2004,[40] or
on December 16th 2005.[41] More optimistic predictions locate
the peak of oil around the 2020s or 2030s, with assumptions
that major investments in fuel alternatives will help to avoid
a peak oil crisis.[42] Jeremy Leggett, though, notes how the
largest oilfields were discovered over half a century ago, with
the peak of oil discovery being 1965. There have been no

major new discoveries since the 1970s. New fields are not being found at the same rate as they were in the now quite distant past. It thus seems a fair estimate that oil production worldwide will have peaked by around 2010.[43]

Energy will be increasingly expensive and there will be frequent shortages, especially as the world's population continues to soar. Both the US Department of Energy and the International Energy Agency suggest that global demand for oil has been increasing by 2 million barrels a day over the last few years. This oil demand could possibly rise from the present level of 86 million barrels a day to 125 within the next two decades, this having to be principally met from Middle Eastern oilfields. However, few Organization of Petroleum Exporting Countries (OPEC) had more production capacity in 2006 compared with 1990. And with Saudi Arabia holding an estimated 22 per cent of global oil reserves, many are sceptical as to whether it is capable of significantly increasing production for this rising demand.

The oil surplus period of the late 1980s and early 1990s led to oil trading at $10 per barrel (in 1998). However, by mid 2008, the price per barrel of oil rose to more than $135. Airlines were beginning to collapse, US car manufacturers were noting reduced sales especially of larger models, and around the world slower driving speeds were recorded.

Geopolitical instabilities in many oil producing countries are thus producing increased fluctuations and destabilizations in oil supply, prices and future energy security. Such fluctuations result in oil price changes that impact almost immediately upon oil-dependent industries. June 2008 saw tens of thousands of Spanish truckers block roads in Spain as well as on the French border. Fuel protests were also seen in the UK, Portugal and France, bringing together varied sectors of the transport industry including truckers and fishermen. Further action across Europe is expected over the changing price of petrol and diesel.[44]

It already is likely that the Arctic Ocean's seabed, which may hold billions of gallons of oil and natural gas (perhaps as much as up to 25 per cent of the world's undiscovered reserves, according to the US Geological Survey), will become the next highly contested energy region. Already in August 2007, Russia planted their flag 2.5 miles (4 km) beneath the North Pole on the ocean bed in an attempt to lay claim to an undersea formation called the Lomonosov Ridge which Russia claims is part of Siberia's shelf.[45] A recent EU Report warns that climate change and the peaking of oil will engender major new conflicts especially in the thawing Arctic.[46]

Similarly, the UK is claiming sovereign rights over a vast area of the remote seabed off Antarctica with an application to the UN covering more than 1 million km^2 (386,000 square miles) of the Antarctic bed.[47] Although the UK claim is in defiance of the 1959 Antarctic Treaty (of which the UK is a signatory), which states that no new claims shall be declared on the continent, it shows how dwindling energy reserves are transforming existing policies and generating newly dangerous conflicts.

A crucial factor impacting upon oil reserves is increasing energy consumption from the developing industrial economies of especially China and India. From 1999 to 2004 China's oil imports doubled. Peak oil researcher James Kunstler estimates that at the current rate of growth in demand China will within 10 years consume 100 per cent of currently available world exports of oil. And this assumes no growth in demand elsewhere in the world and no fall-off in global production.[48] It may be that in a world of globally contested, and diminishing, oil and energy reserves, a 'rush and a push' for remaining resources will ensue. The main industrial states and corporations will try to get their hands on available supplies and secure distribution channels (which is trickier, since many pipelines run through unstable geopolitical regions).

In short, not having sufficient oil to sustain rising levels of global economic growth and consumption will generate significant economic downturns, resource wars and lower population levels. Also, the world's fuel resources are under threat of petro-political blackmail from oil producing states. Heinberg sees peak oil as hitting global energy markets within two decades or less, leading to much potential political and civil unrest. Kunstler considers the systems effects to be dire:

> At peak and just beyond, there is massive potential for system failures of all kinds, social, economic, and political. Peak is quite literally a tipping point. Beyond peak, things unravel and the center does not hold. Beyond peak, all bets are off about civilization's future.[49]

In particular, the worldwide transport sector has a dependency on oil of 98 per cent and this represents approximately 50 per cent of all global oil consumption, about 20 per cent of all energy consumption. This follows an annual average growth rate of more than 2 per cent.[50] The inefficient internal combustion engine is principally fuelled by the primary energy sources of oil, natural gas and coal, producing a combination of petrol/gasoline, diesel and liquefied petroleum gas (LPG). There are many other types of vehicles that rely on fuel: delivery fleets, couriers, taxis, military and so on. The largest fleet of vehicles worldwide is the US Federal Government's with around 600,000 vehicles, and as yet they do not lobby for alternative fuels. More generally, the infrastructures of developed and developing nations are predicated upon the plentiful supply of 'cheap' oil to lubricate many areas of industrial, military and commercial life.

Central, then, to understanding development around the world is to appreciate the significance of black gold and especially the power of its vested interests. Jeremy Leggett describes the 'Empire of Oil' as being 'without doubt the most powerful interest group on the planet', much more powerful than most nation states. Hence, 'The Great Addiction' (to oil) remained with oil becoming vital to virtually everything that is done on the planet.[51] And the oil industry did not consider that they had to think to the future. As one industry leader wrote in 1897: 'As to future generations, we can safely trust them to settle their own difficulties and satisfy their own wants'.[52]

And these oil interests have consistently exaggerated the size of their reserves, upon whose estimates official global figures depend. Recently, they suggested that the peaking of global oil is further away than it is (and have in some cases been leading funders of climate change denial publicity and extensive lobbying).

More generally, American and European foreign policies are driven by global oil interests. In the US, the desire to increase access to oil sources from outside the US since its decline in oil production in the 1970s is the context for its attempted subjugation of Middle Eastern oil interests in the name of 'freedom' (we might add that the freedom here is principally of US citizens to drive).

There is some limited critique of this power of oil, with the European Commission Chief José Manuel Barroso announcing in 2007 that it was time for a 'post-industrial revolution'. In this, the EU would cut greenhouse gases by 20 per cent by 2020[53] but it was simultaneously motivated by Europe's vulnerability as a major oil importer. As a move to secure European self-sufficiency Barroso stated that the EU should look towards supplying 20 per cent of its energy needs from renewable power by 2020, with 10 per cent of vehicle fuel coming from home-produced biofuels. We return in chapter 4 to the significance of transport policies that simultaneously address climate change and energy security.

VIRTUAL WORLDS

We turn now to a third major change in the climate affecting travel and transport. Since around 1990 there has been a remarkable change in the nature of human life itself. There were until then two distinct kinds of things that provided the background to people's everyday lives. First, there was the 'natural world' of rivers, hills, lakes, soil, storms, crops, snow, earth and so on. This physical world provided the taken-for-granted background for almost all of human history. Second, there was the background made up of the 'artificial' objects of the industrial revolution, such as trains, pipes, steam, screws, watches, lights, paper, radio, cars and so on. This background gradually spread around the world, especially during the twentieth century.

But developing from 1990 onwards a new background emerges. This is the world of 'virtual' objects. These include computer and mobile screens, cables, computer mice, signals, satellites, ringtones, texts, sensors, software and so on. In the background of twenty-first century life are virtual objects, hovering and increasingly taken for granted. Some such backgrounds are not simple or fixed but 'smart', sensing, adapting to and transforming lives in a more interactive fashion. Many such virtual objects are only noticed or remarked upon when they break down (which they do).

These virtual objects are predominantly developed and embedded within private sector corporations. They depend on software.[54] They make certain actions seem unexceptional and unproblematic. The software makes it more or less certain that the product can be purchased, the meeting will happen, the hire car is ready and waiting, the components will arrive at the factory, the plane can be boarded, the message will get through, the money will arrive, the friends can be met, and so on. All these mundane actions depend on virtual objects.

According to sociologist Manuel Castells, the growth of micro-electronics-based communications technologies thus transforms the nature of life.[55] It leads from more hierarchical to more horizontal ways of organizing economic and social life. Especially important was the 'invention' of the World Wide Web in 1990, which enables (mostly) seamless jumps from link to link without regard to conventional borders of country, language, subject or discipline. This novel language and architecture initiates an astonishing array of virtual projects, services and sociabilities. With information thus becoming 'digital' it is much less tied to place. Information is everywhere.

Central to human experience then are flickering 'screens' increasingly carried close to or often now on the body. Castells summarizes how:

> What is specific to our world is the extension and augmentation of the body and mind of human subjects in networks of interaction powered by micro-electronics-based, software-operated, communication technologies. These technologies are increasingly diffused throughout the entire realm of human activity by growing miniaturization [and portability].[56]

This digitizing of information has another side. Fears over security and safety have reached unusually high levels in the opening decade of the twenty-first century. These are times of emerging risks, of uncertain 'enemies', that some refer to as a post-millennium state of 'insecurity'. A terror suspect can no longer be easily identified as 'the enemy' and so all civilians can be categorized as 'potential terrorists'. This has been referred to as *Bin Laden in the Suburbs*.[57] Societies are increasingly the 'battle zone' where security issues of surveillance, tracking and identification are played out through new ways of tracking and tracing the movements of populations and increasingly of specific classes of travellers.

This battle zone is especially found at transport hubs. These hubs are where meetings proliferate and travellers are rendered temporarily static. They include airports where biometrics for advanced passenger screening for speedy processing are being trialled (such as Heathrow),[58] or have already been installed (such as at Schiphol). Also currently under development are Radio Frequency Identification (RFID) tagging, soon to be introduced into passengers' tickets and luggage for tracking and monitoring.[59] Security threats will potentially aim to exploit the inherent fragilities of networked mobilities, specifically within the gaps and cracks in urban architecture.[60]

Thus, state policies are much concerned with the security implications of movement. Future transportation will increasingly build digital security into the infrastructure, and these will monitor and regulate 'mobile individuals' and will assess the potential threat of rogue attacks. Transport security and monitoring are thus emerging markets for corporations.[61] Virtual objects are part of the background experience of travel sites, and this we will see is very relevant to developing new systems for personal travel that are 'after the car', that involve locating new virtual objects not only in vehicles, but also in street furniture, roads, lamp posts and so on in major urban centres where much of the world's population now lives, as we shall now explore.

POPULATION AND CITIES

We will now briefly consider the scale and location of the world's growing population. In the late 1990s, the world's population was growing by about 900 million per decade, the largest absolute increases in human history.[62] This is equivalent to a new London every month. By the end of the twentieth century the world population passed 6 billion and is expected to reach 9.1 billion by 2050.

The UN World Urbanization Prospects Report described how the twentieth century witnessed the rapid urbanization of the world's population, as the share living in cities rose from 13 per cent (220 million) in 1900, to 29 per cent (732 million) in 1950, to 49 per cent (3.2 billion) in 2005. The UN report forecast that 60 per cent of the global population will live in cities by 2030.[63] In 2005 urban dwellers already numbered 3.2 billion, about half of the world's population.[64] According to estimates, the world has gone urban, with May 23rd 2007 being 'transition day'.[65] It seems that we now inhabit an 'urban planet'.

Already, modern cities are the largest structures ever created. There are mega-cities such as Tokyo with around 13 million residents (35 million in the Greater Tokyo Area) and Sao Paulo with around 11 million (unofficial estimates are much higher). Future increases will be particularly marked in developing regions which already possess huge populations. These include cities in China, India and parts of Africa. Much of the flow of population around cities comes from refugees, and movements of 'people of concern' as designated by the Office of the UN High Commissioner for Refugees (UNHCR). In 1978, there were fewer than 6 million refugees; by 2005 there were 21 million; and by 2006, 32.9 million.[66] The numbers will rise further as climate change impacts to displace large rural communities, especially in the 'poor south' of the world, generating what has been provocatively termed 'climactic genocide'.[67]

Rapid urbanization in developing countries also exposes large populations to many hazards, such as shortages of clean drinking water and sanitation as well as rising air pollution and air-borne toxins. Most mega-cities within developing countries fail to meet WHO (World Health Organization) standards for air quality. Rising populations also add to the global consumption of energy and raw materials, as well as environmental carrying capacity, leading towards further resource depletion. Today's cities consume three-quarters of the world's energy and are responsible for at least three-quarters of global pollution.[68]

Overall, where cities were once viewed as the cradle of civilization, they now produce disastrous social inequalities, environmental decline and what urbanist Mike Davis terms 'global slums'.[69] He notes how: 'the cities of the future, rather than being made out of glass and steel . . . are instead largely constructed out of crude brick, straw, recycled plastic, cement blocks, and scrap wood . . . much of the twenty-first-century urban world squats in squalor, surrounded by pollution, excrement, and decay'.[70] These are the places of dwelling for at least 1 billion people. And they are also places of death with poor levels of public transportation and hence high use of cars. The result is 'sheer carnage', with 1 million people killed in road accidents each year in Third World cities, many of whom will never own a car in their lifetime.[71]

One of the most astonishing urban projects is China's intention partly to deal with this issue by building 400 new cities within the next 20 years.[72] This will generate the most extensive migration in history. Tens of millions of Chinese will move from rural to urban centres between now and 2050.[73] And it has been estimated by the International

Monetary Fund that the number of cars in China will increase from 21 million in 2005 to a staggering 573 million in 2050; this is part of an almost sixfold global increase over this period.[74] Given the rapid urbanization and industrialization in the emerging markets of Asia and Africa, and especially in China and India, potential car growth is astronomic. If China reaches the US's per capita level of car ownership: 'it would have some 970 millions cars, 50% more than the entire worldwide car fleet in 2003'.[75] In most cities in Africa, Asia and Latin America, the growth in public transport is slower than population growth. If people in these countries, especially on the back of rising economies, also demand 'western' levels of private car ownership, this will place enormous strain on domestic transport infrastructures, road safety, global world fuel resources and the global environment. This was reflected in the very mixed reaction to the exceedingly cheap People's Car to be built by Tata and sold in India in 2008.[76] In China, officials are banning bicycles from some of the busiest urban roads, such as Shanghai. Bicycles are no longer allowed on over fifty major roads especially those where the city's new financial and industrial centres are located.[77]

A world of modern cities based on transport tied to the ubiquitous use of fossil fuels adds to rising social instabilities and presents major challenges. These global cities and their sickening slums will strongly determine the degree, and nature, of future mobilities. To be mobile is increasingly to participate in resource management. As urban environmentalist Herbert Girardet says, today we don't really live in a civilization, but in a 'mobilization' – of natural resources, people and products.[78] In a global world, where many interdependencies and interconnections are mutually based on the stability and maintenance of such systems, there is much room for system vulnerabilities, tipping points and breakdowns (see chapter 3 below). If we are moving after the car, then such a system will need to transform these global mega-cities before they become wholly dominated by the car system.

CONCLUSION

In the next chapter we examine the historic rise of the car and especially how such an 'inefficient' machine became the dominant mode of travel in the fateful twentieth century. We also examine how this car, with its dirty internal combustion engine and massive 1-ton steel body, still continues as a commodity of desire in the twenty-first century and continues to configure so much of the contemporary high carbon world. We then examine in later chapters just whether it is possible to envisage a different system that is 'after the car' and how this could be brought into being within a short period of time, before the forces of global heating have, with speed and violence, set course for an irreversible and catastrophic climate of change. We examine how much the peaking of oil, increasingly ubiquitous virtual objects and the huge concentrations of urban populations could aid the emergence of a system that is after the car.

In a recent semi-popular study, Jared Diamond provides a salutary analysis. He notes how environmental problems have in the past greatly contributed to the 'collapse' of societies.[79] Eight environmental factors were responsible: deforestation and habitat destruction; soil problems; water management problems; over-hunting; over-fishing; effects of introduced species on native species; human population growth; and the increased per capita impact of people.

Diamond then goes on to suggest that four contemporary factors are weakening and potentially causing the collapse of current and future societies: human-caused climate change;

build-up of toxic chemicals in the environment; energy shortages; and full human utilization of the earth's photosynthetic
capacity. The convergence of these factors will produce
abrupt, potentially catastrophic effects.[80] A combination of
increased urbanization, growing resource depletion, population expansion and accelerated climate change will impact
upon twenty-first century societies and constrain the possibilities of re-engineering future mobilities and energy uses
so as to avoid the 'societal collapse' of the sort Diamond
elaborates. But it may already be too late because of those
high carbon societies of the twentieth century and their dev-
astating impacts. They were based on growing populations,
the widespread use of large systems of producing energy, the
growth of huge cities and the taking over of the world by the
car system, as we now examine.

And fighting climate change – that is campaigning not for
abundance but for austerity, not for high consumption but
for low – is a strange politics indeed. It is a politics against
others but especially against oneself and the high carbon
systems that have made life in the rich north nice, comfortable and long. In the final chapter, we examine how climate
change, peak oil and global population growth may well
come to make life 'nasty, brutish, solitary, and short' in the
words of Thomas Hobbes.[81]

2

THE CENTURY OF THE CAR

THE CAR AS 'CIVILIZATION'

Science fiction author and essayist Arthur C. Clarke once wrote that civilization could not survive for ten minutes without the car. Although the car could be improved, it was unlikely to be replaced by anything fundamentally different. Clarke wrote that the world had moved on wheels for 6,000 years, with an unbroken sequence from the ox cart to the Rolls-Royce and Mercedes-Benz.[1] He went on to wonder whether there is anyone still alive who can remember when the situation was otherwise, as the automobile has become so much part of the social world. According to Clarke, the car is an incredible device but one which no sane society would tolerate. It would cause a casual observer on a Monday morning or a Friday evening to conclude that they had entered a living hell.

Similarly, the British poet Heathcote Williams in his book-length poem of car mania called *Autogeddon* notes how aliens from afar observing life on earth would conclude that the major life form was in fact the automobile.[2] It acts as a host to its needy carbon-consuming occupants. Another critic, Kenneth Schneider, remarks in *Autokind Versus Mankind* that 'man' has always had his tragedies. Today, he has the tragedy of the automobile, which is a tragedy of love, and as always, love and necessity are connected.[3] The automobile signifies many of the most troubling aspects of human civilization.

So just how did it come to be? Why and how did the twentieth century become the century of the car? This chapter accounts for why the steel-and-petroleum car came to be the dominant mode of mechanized transport in Europe, the US and then throughout the world. Such a system consists of cars made of steel and weighing about 1 ton, powered by petrol, each seating at least four people, personally owned, and each driven independently of others. This chapter examines how this car system overcomes a public timetable by enabling car drivers to develop their *own* timetabling of social life. We examine how the car becomes central to 'modernism' and is built into modern planning and architecture. The car has configured much contemporary economy, culture, politics and society. We examine how this system of the car came to be 'natural', part of the world that is taken for granted, inevitable, 'locked in' and apparently impossible to escape from.

INTERNAL COMBUSTION

All good histories of invention involve a myriad of inventors, tinkerers and opportunists, mixed with human ingenuity and ideals of progress and problem-solving. The story of the automobile is no exception.[4]

We can begin by noting how battery-powered electric vehicles (BEVs) were among some of the earliest automobiles. Scottish businessman Robert Anderson invented what was effectively the first crude 'electric carriage' between 1832 and 1839. With improvements in the design of storage batteries by Frenchmen Gaston Plante (1865) and Camille Faure (1881), BEVs began to increase, especially in Britain and France. Already, the idea of an automotive future was catching on and inspiring people's imagination, with more than thirty books published on automobiles in the US before 1850.[5]

At first, though, the main centre for automobile development was Europe.[6] A pivotal step came in 1860 when Étienne Lenoir, a Belgian inventor working in Paris, developed an internal combustion engine that resembled a steam engine. The race was, literally, on when Nicholas Otto found a partner in Gottlieb Daimler and together they produced a four-stroke cycle engine in 1876 in the newly unified Germany. At around the same time, Karl Benz began manufacturing a two-stroke engine in 1883.

There was much competition between French and German designers and engineers. In Germany, Daimler and Wilhelm Maybach founded the Daimler Motor Company (DMG) and sold their first car in 1892. In France, Armand Peugeot entered automobile design around 1889 by producing steam-powered tricycles, before buying a number of one-cylinder Daimler engines to fit into a small car produced in 1890. By 1896 Armand Peugeot had set up his own company, Société Anonyme des Automobiles Peugeot, and was concentrating on the manufacture of internal combustion engine cars. With this, Armand Peugeot had established the foundations of the French motor industry.

Thus, we can say that the automobile revolution began around 1890 when car production started rising and inventors in both Europe and North America began to invest in various vehicle production technologies.[7] New innovative automobile designs were appearing using various types of power: steam, gas, electric, and the controversial, and sometimes explosive, petroleum-based internal combustion engine. The central question is how did the potentially dangerous and toxic internal combustion engine become the engine of choice? The answer lies in part at least in public races for these various 'speed machines'.

The first major European public 'road race' was held in 1894 and was a 'competition for horseless carriages' from Paris to Rouen. Of the 102 cars originally entered, only 21 were ready for the trial, including Peugeot cars with Daimler engines, a Roger-Benz car, and several steam cars. Twelve out of the thirteen cars with Daimler engines finished on time, as well as the single Benz, with first prize being awarded to Peugeot and Levassor. However, only one steam car arrived within the time limit, effectively signalling the death of the steam car within the burgeoning automotive industry. Yet a new, more rigorous race was organized a year later from Paris to Bordeaux and back, some 745 miles, with a maximum time limit of 100 hours. In this unprecedented race, twenty-three automobiles left the starting line. Eight of the nine that arrived within the time were petrol powered, developed by Peugeot, Daimler or Benz. This reinforced the dominance of the internal combustion engine for endurance and reliability by comparison with both electric and steam. Thus, by the end of 1895 the automobile developers in Europe had demonstrated that the internal combustion engine car driven on petroleum could be a reliable mode of transport.

In the US, the profile of the car was also being raised by high publicity races, the first being the Chicago Times-Herald race in 1895. The race route was from Chicago to Evanston and back, some 50 miles (80 km). Only two cars crossed the finish line, both petroleum-based. This signalled another nail in the coffin for the horse and carriage and the beginning of the large-scale production of the American petroleum-based automobile.

In 1895, three firms produced almost all the cars in the world. These were Benz in Germany and P & L and Peugeot in France. By 1900, the French factories were producing 4,800 automobiles; Germany 800; Britain about 175; and the US 4,000. Incidentally, it was only in 1896 that Britain finally repealed its 'red flag' laws that required a man on foot to walk in front of each motor vehicle, waving a red flag and often blowing a horn to warn others of the oncoming vehicle.

By 1904–5, US production began to overtake France, reaching 44,000 by 1907.[8] The publicity race between electric and petroleum driven automobiles was getting into full swing. A popular journal of the time – the *Horseless Age* – printed much propaganda and rebuttals from the two fuel-feuding factions. A well read article from April 1896 praised the virtues of the electric car, saying: 'of course, there is absolutely no odour connected with the electric vehicle, while all the gasoline motors we have seen belch forth from their exhaust pipe a continuous stream of partially unconsumed hydrocarbon in the form of a thin smoke with a highly noxious odour'.[9]

The August 1897 New York edition of *Electrical World* observed that it: 'is very evident to the average observer that the so-called horseless carriage is looming up as an important factor in the urban transportation problem'.[10] The electric motor car attempted a massive public relations comeback in light of its defeat in the major European and American road races. A major event occurred in 1899, when the famous auto racer Camille Jenatzy set a new land speed record on the outskirts of Paris in his bullet-shaped electric roadster 'La Jamais Contente'. This was the first car to break the mile-per-minute record by reaching 65.8 mph. In 1900, 28 per cent of American cars were electric.[11]

Early enthusiasm for the electric car was seized upon by the Detroit Electric Car Company, which began production of BEVs, powered by rechargeable lead acid batteries, in 1907. Both Thomas Edison and, interestingly, Henry Ford invested in the company, believing there was a great future for BEVs. In 1911, Edison also introduced his nickel–iron battery to the fleet of production vehicles. The cars were said to be capable of achieving 80 miles (130 km) on a single battery recharge, although top speed was around 20 miles per hour (32 km/h). Yet this could have been considered adequate for city driving at the time.[12]

However, the automobile war was becoming dirty, with fossil fuel driven combustion engine proponents claiming that 'their dirty, noisy, smoky machines were simply the latest obnoxious manifestation of progress . . . a progression of modern machines that were progressively more intrusive, noisome, filthy, and fouling'.[13] Modernity, as in the railroad and now the car, should thus be noisy!

Ransom Olds, who had built his first steam-powered automobile in 1886, switched to internal combustion to compete with the European models and began large-scale production line manufacturing in 1902. This was then famously expanded upon by Henry Ford as he developed and introduced the car assembly line in 1913. The early 1900s thus saw a shift in automobile production from Europe to US. The petrol system came to be established and 'locked in', with the first model T appearing as early as 1908, more or less as the futurist Marinetti was proclaiming the new 'beauty of speed'. US car registrations in the first decade of the twentieth century jumped from 8,000 to 500,000. The development of petrol-fuelled internal combustion engines is a story of US industrial dominance over Europe, and the world, during the fateful early years of the twentieth century.

A further highly significant reason why the petroleum

car came to be dominant was rapid emergence of cheap oil. Oil had first been discovered in the US in Titusville, Pennsylvania in 1859. Further major oilfields were discovered elsewhere in Pennsylvania and then Ohio, with further strikes following in Texas and Oklahoma in 1901. The US came to develop as the world's leading oil producer in the first half of the twentieth century, and this consolidated petroleum as the fuel for the newly emerging car produced under conditions of Fordism.

And the Great War sounded the *final* death knell of the electric car. The internal combustion engine was crucial to the mechanizing of warfare, where speed, durability, and power *on a battlefield* were central to new forms of warfare. As journalist and historian Edwin Black noted: 'the electric moment had been lost. Warfare was too important and the demand for internal combustion too great'.[14] The internal combustion engine and the steel bodied vehicle won two wars; one abroad on European soil, and the other at home in the domestic car market. After this, US automobile production derived from a series of relatively contingent small causes led to its petroleum-based domination. This began in the US, then spread back to western Europe, and then to the rest of the world.

THE INDUSTRIOUS RISE OF THE CAR

The Fordist production and consumption system was thus established at the beginning of the last century.[15] The economic gains accrued from the assembly line meant mass production at low prices and with little choice. And this helped to develop an automobile consumer class in a marketplace hitherto reserved for mostly young wealthy men who treated their cars as 'speed machines'. Now the automobile could become a commodity for the masses and especially for many families living in the American suburbs. These new consumer cars were driven by their owners and not, as was more common in Europe, by professional drivers. And people's homes were increasingly powered by electricity and full of self-operated consumer goods. Electricity and automobility are the two great energy transformations of the American century.[16]

Also, the success of assembly line production gave the US automotive industry a dominant market position that quickly spread worldwide. As the US auto-industry grew, so European car manufacturers such as Citroën and Peugeot adopted assembly line production. By 1930, up to 250 smaller car manufacturers had disappeared because they could not keep up with the latest in efficient production technologies.

The next step within this automotive system was for car manufacturers to start sharing car parts with one another, resulting in larger production volumes at lower costs. The automotive industry has since developed its interrelated network system as part of a global strategy. This is how a complex system best operates (see chapter 3).

The steel-and-petroleum car was also aided by extensive government policies, initially in North America and northern Europe, to build complex networks of paved roads. Although cars had developed by the early 1900s, they did not have suitable places to go to even in the US until extensive paved roads appeared from 1932 onwards, with interstate highways developing after 1956. Road building in inter-war Germany was especially significant, with the National Socialist Party developing the model of car-only roads.[17] Later, as motorways came to be provided for cars in many different societies, so the state began to fund such roads out of general taxation. These were newly designed roads for fast traffic separated from other systems of movement. New road users had to be taught how to be competent users of such new 'driving spaces', such as Britain's M1.[18]

Further, the car system developed significantly through the undermining of alternative systems. Between 1927 and 1955 in the US General Motors, Mack Manufacturing (trucks), Standard Oil (now Exxon), Philips Petroleum, Firestone Tire & Rubber and Greyhound Lines joined in violation of anti-trust laws. These companies shared information, investments and 'activities' in order to eliminate ground transport, especially of streetcars. Each corporation established various front companies in which they invested. One of these front companies was National City Lines (NCL), which along with subsidiaries proceeded to buy up, and then to tear up and destroy, the streetcar lines. The strategy was to control urban transport systems so as to force a shift away from electrified buses and streetcars to motorized petroleum-fuelled transport. Local citizens were left without alternatives other than cars and buses. Only in 1955 was the conspiracy 'found out' and the companies charged with violation of the Sherman Anti-Trust Act and found guilty, but they were only subject to tiny fines.[19]

This conspiracy helped the car rapidly to become a consumer good owned and driven by private individuals (mainly men), offering utopian notions of progress. The car's unrelenting expansion of, and domination over, other systems of movement came to be viewed as natural and inevitable. Nothing, it was thought, should stand in the way of the car's modernizing path and its capacity to eliminate the constraints of time and physical space.

And over the course of the twentieth century, this naturalization of the car was reinforced through the notion that urban environments should be auto-monopolized. The car system is a way of life and not just a means of transport from one place to another. Its distinct characteristics make it

unlike any previous system of movement. Through a number
of interdependent effects the industrious rise of the car cast
its long shadow over the twentieth century.[20]

First, then, cars are the exemplary manufactured objects
produced by the leading business sectors and iconic names
within twentieth-century capitalism – names include
Mercedes, BMW, Jaguar, Rolls-Royce, Toyota, Peugeot-
Citroën, Ford, Mustang, Mini, General Motors, Volkswagen
and so on. And more and more countries are developing
significant automobile industries, such as Brazil, China and
India's rising market share (partly through what is planned
to be the world's cheapest ever car).[21]

Second, the car is in most households the major item of
individual consumption after housing and one becoming ever
more popular with each new generation of young adults. It is
a sign of adulthood, and the basis of sociability and networking. Its large cost does not preclude quite poor households in
many societies gaining access to a car, either owned or bor-
rowed or lent out or illegally accessed.[22] Cars provide status
to their owners through speed, security, safety, sexual success, career achievement, freedom, family and masculinity.
Overall, there are a range of 'automotive emotions' which
are built into owning and possessing a car. Particular models
are objects of desire that are lusted after and worshipped.
These emotions also link to the *freedom* to drive and reinforce anti-state libertarian politics protesting against petrol
taxes or road-user pricing.[23]

Third, the car has very many linkages with other institutions, industries and related occupations. These include
licensing authorities; traffic police; petrol refining and distribution; road-building and maintenance; hotels, roadside
service areas and motels; car sales and repair workshops;
suburban and greenfield house building sites; retailing and
leisure complexes; advertising and marketing; and urban

design and planning. These linkages have helped to spread the system around the world. Huge profits have been associated with those producing and selling the car and its related infrastructure, products and related services.

Fourth, car culture has developed into a dominant culture generating new ideals about what represents the 'good life' and what is necessary to be a good mobile citizen in the twentieth century. It is a veritable *Autopia*. For example, the whole notion of American society, its suburbs, urban strips, and mobile motel culture, is based on a car-based life. Cars have become literary and visual icons, representing the 'on the road' liberation of individualism, exploration and experimentation. Cars are more of a right than a responsibility. And their role as iconic objects has been explored through modernist literary and artistic images in novels by E. M. Forster, Virginia Woolf, Scott Fitzgerald, Daphne du Maurier, Jack Kerouac, John Steinbeck, and J. G. Ballard. The car is also the stylized body for screen presences such as James Dean or Steve McQueen. Iconic car films include *Rolling Stone, Alice Doesn't Live Here Anymore, American Graffiti, Bonnie and Clyde, Vanishing Point, Badlands, Thelma and Louise, Paris, Texas, The Italian Job, Bullitt* and *Crash*.[24]

Fifth, the car driver is increasingly surrounded by control systems that allow a simulation of the domestic environment, a home from home moving flexibly and riskily through strange and dangerous environments. The car is a sanctuary, a zone of protection, however slender, between oneself and that dangerous world of other cars, and between the places of departure and arrival. The driver is strapped into a comfortable, if constraining, armchair and surrounded by micro-electronic informational sources, controls and sources of pleasure. Once in the car, there is almost no movement from the driver. So although automobility is a system of mobility, it necessitates minimal movement once strapped *into* the driving seat. Eyes have to be constantly on the look-out for danger, hands and feet are ready for the next manoeuvre, the body is gripped in a fixed position, lights and noises may indicate that the car driver needs to make instantaneous adjustments, and so on. The other traffic constrains how each car is driven, its speed, direction, its lane and so on. The driver's body is disciplined to the machine, with eyes, ears, hands and feet all trained to respond instantaneously and consistently, while desires even to stretch, to change position, to doze or to look around are suppressed.

And finally, the car system creates massive environmental resource use and an extraordinary scale of death and injuries, of 'car-nage' (the former were outlined in chapter 1). With regard to the latter, the car system produces its own 'negativity', deaths and injuries being many times greater than any previous system. Modern roads are the 'killing fields' of contemporary societies. Crashes have become normal and predictable, typically referred to as 'accidents', aberrations rather than 'normal' features of the system. The book and the film *Crash* examined the dramatically fast deaths and erotic woundings that cars produce.

Worldwide, cars generate 1.2 million deaths and 20–50 million injuries a year, many involving people who are not car drivers. The estimated global cost is $518 billion. Even in relatively 'safe' Europe, more than 30 million people have been injured and/or permanently handicapped over the last 20 years.[25] More than 40,000 people are killed each year in the US. It is estimated that traffic injuries will become the third largest contributor to the global burden of ill-health and physical impairment by 2020.[26] Studies predict that road traffic deaths will increase by 83 per cent in low income and middle income countries, but decrease by 27 per cent in high income countries. Overall, there is a predicted global increase of 67 per cent by 2020.[27] Many deaths occur in China, India,

Thailand, Kuwait and Venezuela. China is said to have 2 per cent of the world's cars but 15 per cent of the world's fatalities.[28]

Given these patterns and other costs of the car, how did such a monster come to take over the world during the last century? The absolutely key feature of the car is its mundane character, its significance for ordinary, everyday social life.

'SOCIALIZING' AUTOMOBILITY

Bertha Benz is often credited with playing a seminal role in turning the machine of the 'car' into a machine for living. In 1885, she took her husband's car out of his workshop where he had been tinkering with it and went for a drive to visit her parents who lived some 80 kilometres away. This is said to be the first *social* use of the car. It required this very striking disruptive innovation, bringing out women's role in initiating new sociabilities. At the time, Benz himself had been concentrating on developing his main business, which was engineering stationary engines. At the time, men mostly conceived of the car as a hobby, as producing 'speed machines' (and often still do today!). Indeed, early cars were less a means of regular movement than a way of demonstrating speed and social superiority over others. These features were reflected in the design characteristics of early European cars.[29]

And yet in the last century automobility became more deeply embedded for its 'social' features and for many people it offers a source of freedom, the 'freedom of the road'. The car's flexibility enables car drivers to get into their car and start it without permission or the expertise of others. It is ready and waiting to spring into life, so enabling people to travel at any time in any direction along the complex road systems that now link most houses, workplaces and leisure sites. Cars extend the possibilities of where people can go to, what they can do and thus who they are.

Much 'social life' could not be undertaken without the flexibilities of the car and its 24 hour availability. It is possible to leave late by car, to miss connections, to travel in a relatively timeless fashion. Automobility thus irreversibly set in motion new flexible socialities, of commuting, family life, community, leisure, the pleasures of movement, its significance in youth culture and so on. Crucial to a lot of car-based sociability is the giving of lifts and the exchanging of favours with colleagues, friends and family. The growth in automobility has involved new kinds of movement, additional journeys and routes, and is much more than the historical replacement of public transport journeys by car journeys. There is a pervasive pattern of car dependence ironically engendered through the ways in which cars enable people's independence.[30]

People thus have come to live their lives through the car and its flexible freedom. As early as 1902 a car driver noted how the car brings into being new temporalities: 'Traveling means utmost free activity, the train however condemns you to passivity . . . the railway squeezes you into a timetable'.[31] The clock time of the modernist railway timetable 'locks one into a cage'.[32] The car system, by contrast, allows liberation from such constraints. As the President of the German Automotive Industry Association pronounced in 1974: 'The automobile is another bit of freedom'.[33] People around the world have come to live their lives through the car and its flexible freedoms.

The seamlessness of the car journey makes other modes of travel seem inflexible and fragmented. So-called public transport rarely provides that seamlessness, since there are many gaps between the various means of public transport, with people experiencing delays and on occasion danger. These 'gaps' are sources of inconvenience, danger and uncertainty, especially for women, children, older people, those who may be subject to racist attacks, the less abled, those travelling at night and so on. By contrast 'security' can be achieved by owning and controlling one's own car, car-cooned in an iron cage away from many of these risks and dangers. The car has been described as a *'secure machine*, a shield against the insecurity of the outside world', and this led in the US to an exceptional turn to the sports utility vehicle (SUV) and the military-derived Hummer.[34]

Many feel they are living through the romantic sense of being *on the road*, experiencing the passing of landscapes or escaping from cities to wide open spaces. Often, these journeys are slow, meandering and do not entail moving from A to B as fast as possible. The car can be linked with the increased significance of a personalized sense of self, a 'self' *on the move* and living in and going with the *flow* of life.[35] But this is of course a very diverse experience marked by major variations in class, gender, ethnicity and age: being 'in the company of cars' varies greatly in terms of skill, emotion, speed, convenience, pleasure and so on.[36]

Thus, the power of automobility is the consequence of its system characteristics. Unlike the bus or train system it is a way of life, an entire culture. It has redefined movement, affect and emotion in the contemporary world. Sheller emphasizes 'the full power of automotive emotions that shape our bodies, homes and nations'.[37]

But the car's flexibility also creates distance and coerces patterns of life. The car separates home, work, business and places of leisure that historically were close together. The car system divides workplaces from homes, producing lengthy commutes into and across the city and stimulating the growth of suburbs. The system splits homes and business districts, undermining local retail outlets to which one might walk or cycle, eroding town centres, non-car pathways and public spaces. It divides homes and leisure sites often only available by motorized travel. Members of families can more easily live apart and out of town, knowing that the car can connect such 'distant places' and re-thread family ties. Cars as a system are a major 'convenience device' of contemporary society, given the distances between where people have come to live. As global architect Richard Rogers writes:

> it is the car which has played the critical role in undermining the cohesive social structure of the city . . . they have eroded the quality of public spaces and have encouraged suburban sprawl . . . the car has made viable the whole concept of dividing everyday activities into compartments, segregating offices, shops and homes.[38]

Living with the car generates the day-to-day juggling of events so as to deal better with the many time constraints that modern life generates. It can be said that the car system is a Janus two-faced creature. Inhabiting the car can be positively viewed in terms of freedom and flexibility; and yet it constrains car 'users' to live their lives in stretched out ways. The car is a motorized, moving and privatized 'iron cage'. People have come to inhabit congested, gridlocked, and health-threatening city environments through being trapped in cocooned, moving iron bubbles.

The 'flow' of flexible car driving – the highways, freeways, autobahns and concrete horizons – exert dominance over surrounding environments and upon people trying to live with the streams of traffic rapidly passing next to their houses. Often, such houses are unsaleable as they are given over to the ruthless car system. This brings about what modernist architect Le Corbusier predicted as an inevitable effect of the movement of traffic, that roads will be monopolized by cars.[39]

And in this single-minded pursuit car travel often interrupts the 'flows' of others (pedestrians, children going to school, postmen, garbage collectors, farmers, animals and so on), whose daily routines are obstacles to the high-speed traffic cutting mercilessly through slower moving routes. Cultural critic Theodor Adorno wrote as early as 1942: 'And which driver is not tempted, merely by the power of the engine, to wipe out the vermin of the street, pedestrians, children and cyclists?'[40] Junctions, roundabouts, sleeping policemen and ramps constitute obstacles to the car drivers who are intent on returning to their normal cruising speed in order to finish their journey on time and especially without delay.

The images and visions of a city 'in modernity' provided by the urban designs of Le Corbusier show the city as a concrete maze, dissected by sharp walled plinths of buildings that reflect the linear consumption of the modern period. In between the towering tablets of office blocks and bridges run the unmistakable dark lines of regulated traffic, moving through the lanes of an urbanized metropolis. And the automobile has come to devour the fabric of such cities like a virulent host. Architect Moshe Safdie has observed how older cities have since had to adapt their city areas to traffic volumes unimagined at the time they were built.[41] He notes how in newer cities, the 'patterns of development, land-use, and land coverage were all determined by the requirements and presumptions of car-dominated transportation from the beginning of their major growth'.[42] As was often the case with the modern city, the straight streets, interspersed with avenues of public spaces, were shaped for the benefit of the auto-car. To construct more roads to fit the need for increasing car use and individualized mobility significantly contributes to 'cities that segregate and brutalise rather than emancipate and civilise'.[43]

The costs of the car, then, go beyond the financial as they

generate multiple social costs for people, habits/lifestyles
and the environment. The twentieth century development
of 'civilized' automobility has inflicted many costs upon the
social world. According to the former (if sexist) Mayor of
Curitiba, Jaime Lerner, cars are our 'mechanical mothers-
in-law', in that 'You have to have a good relationship with
your mother-in-law, but you cannot allow her to conduct
your life'.

FUTURES

In 2000, there were more car owners in the US than registered voters; and in 2002 the average adult in the US made
86 per cent of their travel trips by car and travelled 13,500
miles per person/per year.[44] Similarly, European countries,
with the exception of Denmark and the Netherlands, are
seeing increases in private car ownership and use especially
in ex-communist states such as Poland. Roughly speaking,
we can say that the more neo-liberal the society, the more
there is encouragement of the use of the private car and the
more likely are large highway construction projects.[45]

Likewise, car ownership, along with the *desire* for car
ownership, is increasing in those African and Asian societies that are experiencing population increase and industrial
growth, at the same time that the supply of public transport
is slowing down. If people in these areas, especially on the
back of rising economies, demand 'western' levels of private
car ownership, this will place enormous strain upon domestic transport infrastructures, road safety, global world fuel
resources and the future climate. If China reached the US's
per capita level of car ownership, 'it would have some 970
million cars, 50 per cent more than the entire worldwide
car fleet in 2003' and 'by 2010 it is expected to import half
its oil'.[46] China is now the second largest car market in the

world, with some global companies such as GM finding that expansion in China is offsetting its domestic decline.

Moreover, increases in private car ownership are not necessarily directly linked to personal income or national prosperity. Some cities, such as Bangkok, have lower levels of wealth than neighbouring cities like Tokyo, and yet they have higher levels of car ownership and use.[47] Often, this is explained by state policy initiatives that advantage and support private car ownership over public transport, especially when encouraged by state authorities with vested interests in a national automobile industry. It also demonstrates the power wielded by major automotive corporations with foreign investment incentives.

Also, German researchers have established that each car, taking up an average surface area of six square metres, is 'responsible for 200 square metres of tarmac and concrete and produces some 44.3 tonnes of carbon dioxide throughout its life'.[48] Or as Joni Mitchell famously sings, 'They paved paradise and put up a parking lot'.[49] Further, the typical car requires 680 kg of steel, 230 kg of iron, 90 kg of plastics, 45 kg of rubber and 45 kg of aluminium. And 8,000–28,000 kilowatt hours of energy are needed to produce a single motor vehicle.[50] Each car, then, is not just a separate entity or 'iron cage', but is a node within a broader system of production and consumption, part of a much larger *mobilization*. The environmental impacts of the car stem from its *entire* life cycle and related infrastructure systems, including extraction of raw materials, vehicle production, operation and maintenance, as well as maintenance of the road infrastructure, hospital costs, emotional costs of the many deaths and injuries and so on. The car user does not pay the full cost, since many of these environmental and public health costs are not embedded in car charges. As such, more than the car thus matters.

So to conclude: in the early part of the twentieth century urban historian Lewis Mumford wrote that most western 'metropolises' had encouraged the 'wholesale invasion of the automobile'.[51] They thus suffered from the effects of traffic queues, personal frustrations, excessive noise and polluted air. We have documented just how the twentieth century has enabled this invasion into all the pores of the social body. And in so doing the car has come to be locked together with high energy production and consumption, it has generated extraordinary levels of carbon consumption, resource depletion and the peaking of oil, and transformed human settlements and in a way humans themselves. Mumford, however, went on to say that it is 'human purpose [that] should govern the choice of the means of transportation'; and that what were needed were better transportation *systems*, not just more roads being built.[52]

In the next chapter, we address the issues of such systems, which we think are crucial to understanding how a transformation away from the power of the car could possibly come about. We must learn to think through the idea of 'systems' and not merely through what separate individuals seem to prefer or to want. It is systems that have to change here in order that a low carbon society may emerge out of the ruins of the twentieth century.

3

SYSTEMS

THE CAR SYSTEM

In the previous chapter we showed how the twentieth century came to be based on the dominant car system. We analysed that century as the century of this car system which became 'locked in' and 'drove' out all competitors. Few, if any, societies have been able to escape its awesome dominance.

This system laid down high carbon patterns of producing and consuming travel and transport. And together with other related high carbon systems, this is taking us to a dangerous and uncertain future, as we outlined in chapter 1. This dangerous future of global climate change, the peaking of oil and the growth of huge and unequal cities stems from an array of systems that are like an out-of-control 'juggernaut'. And central to high carbon society is the car system, and other systems such as electricity-based energy.

And it is *systems* we hold that are central to explaining these patterns of climate change, energy insecurity and vast

out-of-control centres of population. But so far, we have not
spelt out what is meant here by this idea of a system.

COMPLEXITY

We will examine the notion of system through some influential developments known as complexity thinking or
complexity sciences.[1] Ideas of complex systems have emerged
in the sciences, and then moved into the social sciences,
humanities and semi-popular writings. Complexity notions
are now found in architecture, consultancy, consumer
design, economics, defence studies, fiction, garden design,
geography, history, literary theory, management education,
organizational studies, philosophy, post-structuralism, sociology, town planning, as well as most of the 'physical sciences'.
Searches of Amazon indicate 1,221 current complexity titles.

So what does the idea of complexity entail? One starting notion is that the physical and social worlds are full
of change, paradox and contradiction. There is no simple
unchanging stable state. There is what science writer Philip
Ball calls 'the strange combination of the unpredictable and
the rule-bound that governs so much of our lives'.[2] Systems
are thus patterned, regular and rule-bound, but through
their workings they can generate unpredictable features and
unintended effects.

Complexity in particular investigates systems that adapt
and evolve as they organize themselves through time. Such
complex social interactions have been likened to walking through a maze whose walls rearrange themselves as
one walks through that maze.[3] New steps have then to be
taken in order to adjust to the walls of the maze that are
adapting to one's movement through it. Complexity thus
investigates emergent, dynamic and self-organizing systems
that co-evolve and adapt in ways that heavily influence the

probabilities of later events. Systems are in process, moving, unpredictable and responding and adapting to their environment. And that environment is itself changing and adapting. Thus, many systems are not in 'balance', stable and unchanging. They depend on external relations with an environment. They receive flows of energy from elsewhere.

In the case of ecological systems, they can receive species from other parts of the globe and also fire, lightning, hurricanes, high winds, ice storms, flash floods, frosts, earthquakes and so on from outside. The 'normal' state is not balance and equilibrium. Populations of many species can demonstrate extreme unevenness, with populations often rising rapidly when introduced into an area and then almost as rapidly collapsing. Thus, there is no essential nature that would be in equilibrium if only humans had not intruded. Any ecological system is immensely complex, so that there are never straightforward policies that restore equilibrium, such as the size of the fish population in a particular ocean.[4] Indeed, actions invariably generate the opposite or almost the opposite from what is intended. So many decisions intended to generate one outcome, because of the operation of a complex system, generate multiple unintended effects often different from what is planned for. A complex world is one of multiple and often unpredictable unintended effects.[5]

So such systems thinking entails getting away from mechanistic ideas and especially away from the idea that systems naturally tend to equilibrium, that stability is the normal state to be in.[6] This complexity thinking characterizes systems as being open and sustained through flows of energy rather than earlier formulations of closed systems that naturally return to equilibrium. So systems are organized, powerful and structured, but they do not naturally or necessarily move to stability.

Such organized systems involve emergent effects where

the interactions between the parts are more fundamental than the parts. Böhm refers to this as the importance of the dance rather than the dancers.[7] It is not that the sum is greater than the size of its parts, but that there are system effects that are different. Complexity examines how components of a system 'spontaneously' develop collective properties or patterns. This includes even simple properties such as colour that do not seem implicit, or at least not implicit in the same way, within individual components. The flavour of sugar is not present in the carbon, hydrogen and oxygen atoms that comprise it. These are non-linear consequences not reducible to the very many individual components that comprise such components.

Many complex systems are characterized by the absence of a central hierarchical structure that 'governs' and produces outcomes. Overall large-scale patterns or characteristics emerge from, but are not reducible to, the micro-dynamics of the phenomenon in question. Thus, gases are not uniform entities but comprise a seething confusion of atoms obeying the laws of quantum mechanics. The laws governing gases derive not from the behaviour of each individual atom but from their statistical patterning.

Physicists Laughlin and Pines thus summarize the shift in thinking involved here. Physics once studied fundamental laws to which everything in the universe – it was thought – could be reduced. Now scientists say it studies multiple forms of organization. They argue that the 'central task . . . is no longer to write down the ultimate equations but rather to catalogue and understand emergent behaviour . . . the study of complex adaptive matter. . . . We are witnessing a transition from . . . reductionism, to the study of complex adaptive matter'.[8] An example of this is the way in which at the nano-scale the laws of physics operate very differently. Molecules at the nano level stick together through self-assembly and hence generate complex nanoscale structures that may well be the basis of new products, industries and forms of life.[9]

Thus, in such systems order and chaos are in a kind of balance where the components are neither fully locked into place but yet do not dissolve into anarchy. There is an 'orderly disorder' present within such dynamic systems. Such systems are unstable and interventions or changes can produce an array of effects. If a system passes a particular threshold with minor changes in controlling variables, switches may occur and the emergent properties turn over. Thus, a liquid turns into a gas, or small temperature increases turn into global heating.[10] This can give rise to unexpected structures and events whose properties are very different from those of the underlying elementary laws.

And the movement from one state to another can be very rapid, with almost nothing in between. These transformations are called phase transitions and the striking thing about them is their abruptness. As a gas is cooled, it remains a gas until it suddenly turns into a liquid.[11] This rapidity of change is also shown in the processes of transformation between each Ice Age and the periods of relative warmth that occur in between. It is argued that there are only two states, the glacial and the interglacial, with no third way, and there has been and will be abrupt movement from one state of the earth's system to the other. Some characterize this pattern as involving 'punctuated equilibria'.[12]

In the social world, this abruptness of change has been formulated in Malcolm Gladwell's notion of tipping points.[13] This involves three notions: that events and phenomena are contagious, that little causes can have big effects, and that changes can happen not in a gradual linear way but dramatically as the system switches overnight.

He describes the consumption of fax machines or (cell) mobile phones, when at a given moment the system switches and suddenly every office needs a fax machine or every mobile person needs a mobile phone. In the US, the tipping point for fax machines was 1987 and for (cell) phones 1998. What is key is that wealth comes here not from scarcity, as in conventional economics, but from abundance. Each fax machine is so much more valuable if every other office also has a fax machine that enables new networked connections to form and extend themselves. The benefits of each extra fax machine are what are often described as non-linear. The tipping point is reached and extraordinary benefits flow throughout the network of offices which all possess the newly fashionable fax machine.

TIME

Central to all the system effects we have just set out is the importance of time and of how systems move through time. Systems are in process.

This significance of time for the very nature and development of systems is particularly shown in thermodynamics. Rather than there being a reversibility of time as held in classical physics, a clear distinction is drawn between what has passed and what lies in the future. There is said to be an arrow of time that results in a loss of organization and an increase in randomness or disorder over time. This accumulation of disorder or entropy results from the Second Law of Thermodynamics. However, there is not a simple growth of disorder. Nobel prize-winning Ilya Prigogine showed how new order arises but is far from equilibrium. What he terms 'dissipative structures', islands of new order within a sea of disorder, maintain or even increase their order at the expense of greater overall entropy. Prigogine describes how such localized order 'floats in disorder'.[14] Open systems exist far from equilibrium and sustain themselves through energy flows. They increase in complexity through an internal generation of networks by using flows of energy from the environment. How an open system responds to the energy inputs shows whether it adapts to new circumstances in terms of growth, or whether it collapses. Some such complex systems, Prigogine observed, 'may evolve spontaneously to a state of *increased complexity*'.[15] Complexity, then, is a process whereby open systems self-organize and adapt in response to fluctuating external conditions.

There is thus an arrow or flow of time that results in futures that are unstable, relatively unpredictable and characterized by various possibilities. Time is both multiple and unpredictable. Prigogine talks of the 'end of certainty' as the complexity sciences overcome what he calls the alienating images of a deterministic world and an arbitrary world of pure chance.[16]

The irreversibility of time can also be seen in the expansion of the universe following the singular event of the 'big bang' creation of the universe 15 billion or so years ago. The scientific discovery of the big bang cannot be reconciled with laws of the physical world that presume that time is reversible, deterministic and involving 'classes of phenomena'. The big bang is a one-off phenomenon like nothing else ever occuring within the known universe. Laws of nature are thus historical and not universal, much more like laws of history.

In systems, then, time flows with minor changes in the past being able to produce potentially large effects in the present or future. Such small events are not 'forgotten'. The branch of complexity called chaos theory involves the rejection of the common-sense notion that only large changes in causes produce large changes in effects. Following a deterministic set of rules, unpredictable yet patterned results can be generated, with small causes generating large effects and vice versa. The classic example is the butterfly effect accidentally discovered by Lorenz in 1961. It was shown that minuscule changes at one location can produce, if modelled by three coupled non-linear equations, very large weather effects very distant from the original site. Nicholas Stern of the Stern Review likewise talks of the 'non-linear nature of weather systems'.[17] In such systems, small changes in driving variables or inputs – magnified by feedback – can produce disproportionate system outcomes.

We have thus set out some general characteristics of systems thinking, which we will use in thinking through the car system and its possible futures. We consider now some more precise mechanisms that generate different paths along which systems may move.

PATHS

Central to explaining how systems are in process is the analysis of feedback mechanisms. In early systems, research in the post-Second World War period analysis mainly focused on negative feedback loops that restored the functioning of whatever system was under examination. Such systems of circular causality involved the processing of information that resulted in re-establishing equilibrium through various kinds of negative feedback. The ways in which a central heating system maintains a room within a given range of temperatures involves such negative feedback loops.

However, in later systems formulations, of complexity, positive feedback loops are examined. These can exacerbate initial stresses in the system, so rendering it unable to absorb shocks and re-establish equilibrium. Positive feedback occurs when a change tendency is reinforced rather than dampened down, as with negative feedback loops. Prigogine and Isabelle Stengers state that 'in such a state certain fluctuations, instead of regressing, may be amplified, and invade the entire system, compelling it to evolve towards a new regime'.[18]

A particularly important form of positive feedback relevant to the economy and society is the notion of 'increasing returns' developed by complexity economist Brian Arthur.[19] This differs from what economists have normally understood by the notion of 'increasing economies of scale'. These economies are those that result from and are found within a *single* organization, such as Ford. These economies within such single firms increase output and over a long time reduce the average costs of production, until such a point that no further gains are possible.

By contrast, the notion of 'increasing returns' involves exponential increases in output (and rewards and wealth) that are spread throughout a network of relationships within which many enterprises are located and operate. These 'externalities' across the network can generate spectacular non-linear increases in output and income, as happened with the overnight adoption of the fax machine. The 'networked economy' changes how economies and their rewards operate, on occasions spreading huge, non-linear gains and benefits. There are increasing returns that result from improved coordination between entities and from the processes of organizational learning across the network. The twentieth-century growth of the externalities involved in the spread of the car system is one of the most striking historical examples of such increasing returns.

Likewise, the internet revolution emerged out of the 'small' local invention of the first Web browser in 1993 and the unpredicted emergence of worldwide e-commerce. This emergence was fuelled by the break-up over the previous decade of existing regional and national markets and the proliferation of new networks, as Manuel Castells describes.[20] Over time, networks may bear no tendency to equilibrium because of the importance of positive feedback. Dynamic and irreversible change takes place over time, change that irreversibly and unpredictably takes a system further from equilibrium. Increasing returns thus involve a complexity-type analysis of positive feedback mechanisms.

Such increasing returns are connected with how patterns of socio-technical development can be 'path-dependent'. The notion of path dependence emphasizes the importance over time of the ordering of events or processes. Unlike linear models, the historical patterning in which events or processes occur significantly influences the way they eventually turn out. Causation can flow from contingent minor events to hugely powerful general processes. Through increasing returns they then become locked in over lengthy periods of time. Thus, 'history matters' in such path-dependent development.

This path dependence is typically established for small-scale, local reasons. Thus, it is said that the QWERTY typewriter keyboard was introduced in 1873 in order to slow down typists and make them less efficient. The typewriter keys would not jam if typists typed more slowly. Hence, letters likely to be used together were distributed at some distance from each other. However, having established this layout for small-scale reasons in the late nineteenth century, this system has remained despite the massive technological changes in what comprises a 'keyboard' during the twentieth century.[21] Likewise, with the introduction of video-cassette recorders (VCRs) the VHS format defeated Sony's Betamax version, although it is generally reckoned to be inferior. It is argued that video rental stores observed that more people had VHS players and stocked up on VHS tapes; this in turn led other people to buy VHS players, and so on until there was complete 'vendor lock-in' to the VHS system.[22]

And from the viewpoint of this book, many argue that

battery forms of powering cars were the most 'efficient' at the turn of the twentieth century.[23] However, as we saw in the last chapter petroleum-based cars came to dominate over alternatives, although they were almost certainly less efficient *at the time*. But the 'path dependence' of the petroleum-based car got locked in. And having got locked in, the rest is history, as an astonishing array of other industries, activities, interests and sociabilities came to mobilize around the petroleum-based car.

Overall, what is key according to Brian Arthur is that 'small chance events become magnified by positive feedback' and this 'locks in' such systems so that massive increasing returns or positive feedback result over time.[24] Relatively deterministic patterns of inertia reinforce established patterns through processes of positive feedback. This escalates change through a 'lock-in' that takes the system away from 'equilibrium' and what could have been optimal in 'efficiency' terms. Douglas North writes more generally: 'Once a development path is set on a particular course, the network externalities, the learning process of organizations, and the historically derived subjective modelling of the issues reinforce the course'.[25] This lock-in means that institutions matter a great deal to the way in which systems develop. Such institutions can produce a long-term irreversibility that is 'both more predictable and more difficult to reverse'.[26] The effects of the petroleum car over a century after its chance establishment demonstrate how difficult it is to reverse such locked-in institutional processes.

Thus, while change is often viewed as the normal order of things, there are certain systems that come to be stabilized for very long periods of time. These systems are path-dependent. An array of events and processes are 'locked into' a reinforcing pattern that affects behaviour, products, industries and forms of social life for decades. Social life, in particular, came to be irreversibly connected to the mode of mobility that automobility both generates and presupposes. This mode of mobility is neither socially necessary nor inevitable but seems impossible to break from. From relatively small causes an irreversible pattern was laid down that has ensured the preconditions for the car's self-expansion over the past 'century of the car'. For path dependency, only certain small causes may be necessary to prompt or tip the initiation of the original 'path'. Such small causes are mostly unpredictable and difficult to foresee, although in hindsight they appear explicable in terms of how they tipped the system into a new pattern. The importance of these small but potentially highly fateful changes has recently been described through the theory of black swans. Such black swans are rare, unexpected and highly improbable, and yet can have huge impacts. They are outliers, not averages. And according to Nassim Taleb, black swans are responsible for much economic, social and political change in the world.[27] They are responsible for making history not crawl but jump.

Such jumps result from processes of positive feedback in response to unexpected small events. They escalate change through a 'lock-in' that over time takes systems away from 'equilibrium'. As outlined in the previous chapter, once established, the petrol-based car system got locked in. Small causes occurring in a certain order at the end of the nineteenth century turned out to have irreversible consequences for the twentieth century. Moreover, this car system changes the environment or fitness landscape for all other existing and future systems.[28] It achieves this through its superior capacities to adapt and evolve by comparison with other mobility systems. It adapts as it spreads along the paths and roads of each society so that it becomes central to, and locked in with, the leading economic sectors and social patterns of twentieth-century capitalism. It promotes the notion of convenience rather than speed, and seems to provide the solution to the problems of congestion that it itself generates. It is central to the individualist, consumerist culture of contemporary capitalism. Unlike the bus or train system, the car system is a way of life, an entire culture. It has redefined movement, pleasure and emotion in the contemporary world, transforming the fitness landscape for all other mobility systems that have to find their place within a landscape predominantly sculpted by the car system.

CHANGING SYSTEMS

Moreover, because of the complex interdependencies of systems it is almost impossible to predict what would effect change in such a system. There are just so many unintended consequences in terms of economic, social and political innovation; and these consequences themselves engender further adaptive and evolving system consequences. And anyway, not all changes. So, how to develop predictions and scenarios of alternative systems futures?

The system that especially concerns us in this book is the car system, where one might predict that whatever else happens it is here for the foreseeable future, precisely because of the path-dependent lock-in we have just described. However, two other key components of complexity thinking can be drawn upon here in order to figure out what different futures for this system might look like.

First, in the history of any systems there are moments of heightened openness, when the die is less cast and various futures are structurally possible. It is not that such change is uncaused but it is less reducible to pre-existing systems, and there is less lock-in. Systems theorist Ervin Laszlo refers to there being certain momentous 'chaos points' when systems may tip from one path to another.[29] And as change happens, it may not be gradual but can occur dramatically, at a moment, in a kind of rush.[30] If a system passes a particular threshold, switches or tipping points occur through new positive feedback and dynamic change. The system turns over, as with the internet growing dramatically in the late 1990s as countless people and organizations adapted and co-evolved with it; or where minor increases in global temperature may provoke out-of-control global heating as noted in chapter 1. So there can be 'chaos points'.

Second, complex systems can exist in a state of 'self-organized criticality', a relatively recent innovation in complexity thinking. If we consider a pile of sand, if an extra grain of sand is added to it there is no telling what will happen. The new grain may simply sit in its place, helping to strengthen the sand pile, or alternatively it may generate an avalanche of sand down the side of the pile.[31] Certain systems can be seen as hovering in a state of such precarious stability, a critical state, neither fully secure nor fully insecure. In conditions of self-organized criticality, what matters is not the average behaviour of elements, people or institutions but what happens at the extreme, such as the last grain of sand that is added to the pile which may tip the avalanche. So in this analysis, what is key is the extreme behaviour of certain components and not the average.[32]

And it is the extreme behaviour, the black swan, which is crucial to the possible transformations of the car system. What we examine in the next chapters is how the car system has for various reasons moved into a chaos point, a state of self-organized criticality. It is neither fully secure nor fully insecure. It may get transformed, but only because of some extreme changes that could unpredictably tip it into an alternative. Predicting the grain of sand that could produce the avalanche rather than the re-established sand pile is impossible. But thinking through the complexity lens enables us to get closer to which small changes at the extreme may just provoke the equivalent of the avalanche for the current car system. And it will be this small change(s) that will mean that the current car system, which currently seems so locked in and stable, can actually be washed away like a pile of sand. When that happens during this current century is central to determining the future configurations of life on planet earth.

4

TECHNOLOGIES

the problems created by the prevalent way of thinking cannot be solved by the same way of thinking. This is a crucial insight. Without renewing our culture and consciousness we will be unable to transform today's dominant civilization and overcome the problems generated by its shortsighted mechanistic and manipulative thinking.[1]

Ervin László, *The Chaos Point: The World at the Crossroads.* (Virginia: Hampton Roads, 2006), p. 39.

INTRODUCING THE NEW SYSTEM

As we outlined in chapter 2, the current car system seems remarkably stable and unchanging. It is reproduced through an extensive economic, social and technological network of vested interests, agents and flows. Well over a century old, and increasingly archaic because of its dependence on oil-based combustion, the car system is able to 'drive' out competitors, of bikes, buses, feet and trains. The twentieth century saw many homes and garages in the rich north filled with the latest electrical and digital gadgets, and yet they sat alongside the oddly outdated petroleum-powered car.

However, we believe that many important technical-economic, policy and social changes are sowing the seeds of a new mobility which will develop in this century. If these changes occur in the next decade or so, then a turning point could be reached. If they are realized in the 'right order', which we can only know in retrospect, they could 'tip' the car system into a new 'post-car system' within the new few decades. This would constitute a major shift into a low carbon alternative to the current high carbon mobility system.

We examine the car system as being made up of humans (drivers, passengers, pedestrians), machines, materials, fuel, roads, buildings and cultures.[2] What is key is not the 'car' but its *system* of connections, as we outlined in chapter 2. This system is set for change due to an array of emerging interdependent processes. The current car system will shift because of changes in this 'mix' of relations. These changes are multiple and our claim is that no single change will be of significance. What is important is transformation to a new *system* of relations, although this may well be provoked by an extreme 'black swan'.

This argument is clarified by innovation expert Frank Geels. He argues that such system innovations 'are not merely about changes in technical products, but also about policy, user practices, infrastructure, industry structures and symbolic meaning, etc.'.[3] Thus, system changes of this sort have a number of characteristics to be demonstrated below: co-evolution of numerous interrelated elements; changes in both demand *and* supply sides; a large range of actors involved; long-term processes stretching over decades; and the sheer impossibility of change being brought about by a single 'policy'.

In emphasizing the system change needed here, we are asserting that changing prices or tax rates or a technological fix will not in themselves generate a post-car future but as part of a broader set of transformations they may be significant. Shifts from one system to another will always involve a complex set of transformations. Mimi Sheller writes:

> Car consumption is never simply about rational economic choices, but is as much about aesthetic, emotional and sensory responses to driving, as well as patterns of kinship, sociability, habitation and work.[4]

A post-car system will need to be at least as effective as the current car at meeting people's economic, aesthetic, emotional, sensory and sociability requirements. This is a tall order.

The following is a diagrammatic representation of what a new 'vehicle system' might consist of. The (figure 4.1) diagram is meant to convey the 'system' quality of any change. In this chapter, we deal mainly with the 'technological' characteristics of such a system (the right-hand side of the diagram) and in the next chapter the more social and 'organizational' features (the left-hand side). In chapters 6 and 7, we consider some examples and prototypes of its development, the conditions under which such a system might materialize and its potential consequences for different futures more generally upon planet earth.

NEW FUEL SYSTEMS

We begin with fuel, but not because this is necessarily the most important component. However, there are some impor-

Figure 4.1 Diagrammatic representation of a new 'vehicle system'.

tant cleaner and more efficient vehicle engines developing that could help to shift away from fossil fuel dependency. As noted in chapter 1, such dependency is not only detrimental to the climate but also serves to sustain resource wars and corrupt states and corporations.

Given the peaking of oil as discussed in chapter 1, fossil fuels will not power the majority of individually driven 'vehicles' by the end of this century.[5] There are various alternatives under development including biofuels, hybrid vehicles, electric batteries and hydrogen. However, each alternative is fraught with conflict and uncertainty. Our thesis here is that one of these will be the basis of personal vehicle movement within a few decades, but which will win out is so far unclear. In part, this is because they depend on how each intersects with the other components of the new system coming into play, assuming, that is, that the worst effects of climate change have not dramatically intervened first and precluded large-scale mass movement (as suggested in two of the three scenarios outlined in chapter 7).

First, there are biofuels, fuels that directly derive from biological sources. This generic definition is, however, misleading in that true biofuels are produced from waste such as biogas from manure or landfill or waste vegetable oil.[6] Their development is thus far limited.

Currently, the main form of 'biofuels' are made from crops and trees grown specifically for that purpose on large-scale plantations. These agro-fuels can be produced from cereals, grains, sugar crops and other starches. These can either be used in their pure state or blended with other fuels. Also oilseed crops, such as sunflower, rape seeds, soy, palm and jatropha can be converted into biodiesel to be used on its own or blended with conventional diesel.

Cellulosic materials, such as various waste products from crops (including grasses, trees and wood) can be broken down with enzymes and turned into bio-ethanol. There are also new breeds of biodiesel technologies, such as the Fischer–Tropsch process, that can synthesize diesel fuels from different bio-masses via gasification.[7] At present, bio-ethanol is the most widely used form of agro-fuel, accounting for 94 per cent worldwide in 2006. Bio-ethanol can be produced from a number of crops including sugar cane, sugar beet, barley, corn/maize, grain and cotton.

Three countries that have developed substantial agro-fuel programmes are Brazil (ethanol from sugar cane), US and Russia (methanol from eucalyptus). The worldwide production of ethanol is 37 million tons, 80 per cent being used as fuel. In 2005 the largest producer of ethanol was Brazil at 37 per cent, with North America at 36 per cent, Asia at 15 per cent, Europe at 2 per cent (others at 15 per cent). The production of ethanol for fuel grew 15 per cent 2000–5, with estimated worldwide ethanol fuel use in 2050–2100 expected to be 33 per cent of the total.[8] Although Brazil has been the world's largest bio-ethanol producer, the USA took over as the leading producer in 2006. Brazil's agro-fuels network has been actively developed and endorsed for decades by a governmental policy with an established history of mixing bio-ethanol with petrol. China is a new player in agro-fuels production, yet is developing fast, partly because of its rapidly growing car market. Currently, China is engaged in agro-fuel plant construction and has established the world's largest agro-fuel ethanol facility at Jilin.[9] In 2007, China announced further plans to set aside 13.3 million hectares of land (mainly in Yunnan and Sichuan provinces) to grow oilseeds and to increase biodiesel production to 10 million tonnes by 2020.[10]

Germany, France and Italy dominate agro-fuel production in Europe.[11] Most EU biodiesel is produced from rapeseed, accounting for nearly 80 per cent. A recent EU report concluded that by 2030 it should supply up to 25 per cent of its transport fuel by clean and CO_2-efficient agro-fuels.[12] Canada, Columbia, India and Thailand have also recently set targets for increasing their national agro-fuel production. Agro-fuels are already big business.

This recent growth in agro-fuels developed for various reasons. These include the increased significance of climate change and 'peak oil' as bases for new international policy discussions; national security concerns with states reducing their dependence on foreign oil and unstable fuel-exporting regions; mass consumer awareness in part generated by rising oil prices; and crises in agricultural production and the need for alternative profitable uses of agricultural land.

These agro-fuels use the existing petroleum infrastructure, which is not the case for other alternative fuels. A globally integrated agro-fuel network can be integrated with the already established global networks of fossil fuel.[13] However, because of this many activists and non-governmental organizations (NGOs) contest the current corporate agro-fuel investments, which they see as reproducing or even worsening existing carbon-based forms of transport.

Corporate interests in agro-fuel production maintain, however, that only a heavily invested globalization of the agro-fuel network can significantly impact on climate change and energy security. However, the focus on the national and corporate industrialization of agro-fuels is creating centralized agro-fuel regions at the expense of local crops and agricultural producers. Thus, large agribusiness companies such as Cargill and Archer Daniels Midland, conventional oil companies such as Total and Shell, as well as car companies such as Toyota and Daimler–Chrysler, are emerging as powerful players.[14] These major players have the resources to secure government subsidies in developed and especially developing countries.

While agro-fuels were once heralded as a panacea for fossil fuel dependency, their production is increasingly seen as problematic. A UN expert recently condemned the growing use of crops to produce agro-fuels as a 'crime against humanity'. The production of agro-fuels has helped to push the price of some crops to record levels and will create additional hunger in developing countries.[15] The UN has also warned that up to 60 million indigenous people may soon be agro-fuel refugees, with tens of thousands of rural families already displaced from their land by soya/agro-fuel companies.[16]

Some of the major problems and limitations of agro-fuels are therefore as follows.

- Increased shortage of agricultural crop land. For either the US or Europe to replace 10 per cent of their present transport fuels using today's technologies would require up to 40 per cent of current crop land.[17]

- Greater environmental problems of deforestation and land degradation, decrease in biodiversity, and water pollution. Increased crop-spraying emits polluting levels of nitrous oxide.
- More damage to food supplies and increased food prices and food scarcity. This is especially significant for developing countries and will lead to increased hunger, malnutrition and poverty.
- Domination of the agro-fuels market by large corporations, leading to the prioritizing of 'cosmopolitan' issues such as climate change and peak oil rather than more immediate local concerns such as water and soil degradation.[18]
- Greater likelihood of corporate land-grab, mostly in the poorer south, that will result in major rises in agro-fuel refugees, possibly in the millions.
- Limited energy output from ethanol. It may be less than the energy required for its production; according to some research it takes 1.29 gallons of petrol to produce 1 gallon of ethanol.[19]

We have spent some time on first-generation biofuels because of their contemporary importance. They are in some ways the ideal neo-liberal solution for climate change and mobility. It is a linear solution, correcting one aspect through identifying a huge new market opportunity, especially for North American agricultural producers with very large acreages that can be easily converted to agro-fuels.

A different agro-fuel manufacturing process uses cellulosic energy crops, such as switchgrass, poplar and other fast growing plants. These 'next-generation' cellulosic biomass feedstock would lessen the strain placed upon standard agricultural land crops.[20] Butanol is currently a potential second-generation biofuel produced by fermentation from a range of organic material, such as molasses left behind by sugar production or whey from cheese production. Butanol has several advantages over ethanol in terms of higher energy output and being easily blended with diesel. Also, because it is less subject to evaporation it is easier to transport. New 'second-generation' bio/agro-fuels are more favourably viewed, although they require advanced technical processes, higher capital investment and larger facilities. This may make them too expensive, especially for developing countries.

Although agro-fuels represent the most high-profile and commercially viable alternative to fossil fuel, it may take two decades or more before they seriously impact on the global oil economy. In the end, this may be nothing more than a global agro-fuels network substituting one institutional arrangement for another without significant long-term transformation. Agro-fuels could become the new fought-over commodity, turning a potential low carbon product into another security contestation. This outcome could result from agro-fuels being turned into large-scale production and overshadowing more localized and distributed forms. Thus, the biofuels market would be better considered in terms of scale, with smaller community schemes proving beneficial to rural communities with a supply of recyclable waste as well as the need to power vehicles such as farming motors. The issue, then, may not be whether biofuels are good or bad, but rather the scale and context of their use, so that biofuel schemes could be located within sustainable programmes focusing on novel uses of waste rather than the move to homogenized forms of large-scale agro-fuel production and cropping patterns. This would involve a move from mass production to distributed and localized schemes, which would aid many communities.[21]

However, there are other new fuel technologies that involve not only a fuel shift but also an engineering shift. This happens with any move from the combustion engine towards electric and hybrid-electric vehicles, fuel cells and lithium batteries. It is these potentially more systemic changes that we now examine.

Hybrid-electric vehicles (HEVs) are a short-term alternative to fossil fuel. HEVs involve a hybrid engine that combines regular petrol-combustion driven mechanical drives with battery driven electrical drives. Usually, the HEV uses the petrol part for long-range driving, switching to battery-electrical power assistance for initial acceleration and low-speed driving conditions. HEV batteries do not require constant recharging as in electric vehicles, since they rely on a long-life battery cell and recharging via the vehicle's kinetic motion and braking. Toyota has captured a niche in the HEV car market with their Prius, and their range is soon to be expanded. Several manufacturers are now entering the HEV market with high-profile 'green' cars, noticeably Honda, GM and Ford. HEVs are considered a 'safe bet' should future fuel cell vehicles fail to become commercial.[22] They can now deliver in some cases 100 miles to the gallon.

An increasingly popular variant of the HEV is the plug-in hybrid-electric vehicle (PHEV). PHEVs are grid-connectable hybrid-electric vehicles that are said to consume 50–90 per cent less of any conventional fuel. The PHEV is the basis for a viable vehicle-to-grid (V2G), distributed generation (DG) system. Here, the car can be plugged back into the grid when not in use, not only to recharge but also to return some of its unused energy during peak demand, for which the owner is reimbursed.[23] In this way, credit can be earned which also encourages non-peak-time driving. This peer-to-peer grid connectivity mirrors the web-like infrastructure of the internet and allows for distributed participation.

A niche market has grown up around these vehicles as boutique eco-iconic motors, with an entrepreneurial industry developing in Silicon Valley, California, partly replacing its once thriving computer industry. It may be that a growing market for plug-in electric vehicles from other than the regular automotive industry could influence the adoption of alternative fuel vehicles. If an infrastructure of recharging stations were developed, a potential tipping point, or system shift, could be triggered. Together with new developments in fuel-driven car batteries, the plug-in hybrid is close to being commercially possible. Toyota has recently announced that it will develop a fleet of plug-in hybrids that run on lithium-ion batteries, instead of the nickel-metal hydride batteries that currently power its Prius and other models.[24]

Current research into new fuel sources such as lithium-ion batteries that are cheaper and more efficient than present car batteries could generate a tipping point. Several leading research institutes are currently developing these alternative batteries, such as a new lithium battery containing manganese and nickel, which is cheaper than the regularly used cobalt.[25] Researchers have modified the battery so that the lithium ions are capable of carrying the battery's charge and making battery recharge up to ten times faster. The process still needs to be made cheaper, however, before it will be commercially produced on a large scale and sufficient economies of scale are generated. An early example of such a car is the Nissan Hypermini (with, incidentally, an aluminium body).

Another recent breakthrough has been made by Toshiba, which unveiled its 'Super Charge ion Battery' (SCiB). This can recharge to 90 per cent of its full capacity in less than 5 minutes and has a life cycle of over 10 years. Toshiba began shipping the SCiB quick-charging battery in 2008 for use in electric bicycles, motorcycles, forklifts and construction machinery. Toshiba expects the new lithium-ion battery will eventually be used in hybrid and electric cars.[26]

With new and improved battery technology, it seems likely that within a decade batteries will be sufficiently advanced to provide energy for personal vehicles. Examples here also include smaller niche engineering firms entering the electric car market. The Swiss firm Kruspan Engineering has developed a modified electric minicar with lithium polymer (LiPo) cells giving the car a single-charge range of 350–400 km (217–249 miles) and a full speed of around 130 km/h (81 mph).

Similarly, emerging technologies are pointing towards new automotive fuel cells that are smaller, lower-temperature versions of solid-oxide fuel cells originally developed for power plants.[27]

Although many of these developments are still some way off commercial production, there is a growing market in electric vehicles using current battery technology. Examples include TH!NK City, Lightning Citroën Saxo and G-Wiz electric cars. Sometimes these are part of car hire schemes as in Jersey, Tokyo and Liselec in France. The World Wildlife Fund for nature argues: 'Automotive transport is ripe for transformational change. . . . The electrification of automotive transport offers a promising way to achieve this objective'.[28] Indeed, states wishing to lessen their dependency on oil are moving towards electric cars. Israel is expecting to become a regional pilot for electrically powered cars.[29] There could be 100,000 electric cars in Israel by 2010, according to Israel Corp's statement to invest $100 million in the project.

Also, commercial delivery companies are examining the potential benefits of electric-powered fleets. Smith Electric Vehicles, the world's largest manufacturer of road-going electric vans and trucks, recently introduced the Newton electric truck into the US. Fully charged, the vehicle has a range of up to 150 miles, while the regenerative braking system returns power to the batteries every time the vehicle slows down or stops. The company also plans to establish from 2010 a major production facility in the US with the capacity to produce up to 10,000 electric trucks per year.

Similarly, a UK-based electric truck manufacturer, Modec, produces the Modec electric truck with a range of up to 100 miles, speeds up to 50 mph, and a payload up to 4,500 lbs. The Modec, like the Newton truck, uses a Zebra sodium nickel chloride battery, although both Modec and Smith Electric Vehicles are working with lithium-ion batteries for the future.

Finally, the major alternative to fossil fuel now being developed by large corporate and alternative sectors is the hydrogen fuel cell and the shift to a full-blown hydrogen economy.[30] The history of hydrogen as a fuel is rich in both innovation and failure. In 1839, Welsh physicist Sir William Grove invented a rudimentary hydrogen fuel cell that produced electrical current from hydrogen and oxygen from an electrolyte. Yet the most significant use of hydrogen was as a lighter than air gas for the Zeppelin airships, made famous by the *Hindenburg* explosion over Lakehurst, New Jersey in 1937.[31] The Nazis continued to experiment with the uses of hydrogen derivatives and used hydrogen-treated coal to create synthetic fuel, building around 1000 motor vehicles powered by hydrogenated coal synfuels.[32] By 1939, more than 92 per cent of Germany's aviation fuel and most of its land vehicle fuel was generated by a coal-hydrogen process.

However, the contemporary use of hydrogen is through energy storage, and in the use of clean fuel cells. Some consider the hydrogen fuel cell car is the 'dream ticket' for the clean vehicle of the future. The hydrogen fuel cell is basically a box that takes in hydrogen and oxygen and produces electricity and water. A UK Government White Paper places the time frame for successful adoption of hydrogen fuel cell cars as 2020.[33] GM, however, have announced that they hope to be producing fuel cell cars by 2010 and that eventually these will be powered by hydrogen. Fuel cells, which convert energy from a chemical reaction and produce electricity similar to batteries, promise a clean car future and near-zero road emissions. Unlike batteries, fuel cells never need to be recharged and will produce energy for as long as the fuel is provided. There are a number of hydrogen fuel cell powered buses – in Hamburg, London and Reykjavik (Iceland has announced itself as the first hydrogen society).

These cells convert hydrogen into electricity once various production, storage and distribution problems are solved. But this is where the problems arise. The type of fuel cell suited for transport is known as a proton exchange membrane fuel cell and requires very pure hydrogen. Current models, however, supply the hydrogen from converted natural gas or petrol with the best energy efficiency of around 35–40 per cent, similar to an internal combustion engine.[34] To overcome this, hydrogen need not be converted in the fuel cell but can be delivered, or 'pumped', directly at filling stations. This, though, requires a whole new production and distribution infrastructure. Hydrogen is a low-density and volatile fuel. And unlike an agro-fuels network, hydrogen would be unable to use existing pipeline distribution infrastructure. Hydrogen, being highly corrosive, can make pipelines brittle. Thus, a new infrastructure system has to be established using suitable materials. The pipelines would also need to allow for high leakage and the tendency of hydrogen to evaporate.

A more suitable way to transport hydrogen would be by tankers carrying it in a liquefied form but, because liquefaction occurs at -253°C, refrigerating the gas to achieve this would be, in the words of one environmentalist, an 'economic nightmare'.[35] On top of this there would be increased haulage traffic. There are also further problems with on-board storage of hydrogen, as hydrogen easily evaporates and must be stored in cylinders that may need to be much larger than any existing petrol tanks. At room temperature, hydrogen takes up much more space than normal petrol fuel. These cylinders would contain a gas prone to leaking and they would need to withstand all imaginable high-impact crashes.[36]

Moreover, while hydrogen has to be stored, the other issue is how it is to be produced. Currently, the costs of producing hydrogen from renewable energy sources are extremely high and likely to remain so for the next few decades. Other reports estimate that renewable hydrogen will not be available for use in fuel cell cars for up to 30 years.[37] As energy writer Richard Heinberg has noted, those on the planet need a solution now and not decades from now.[38] Hydrogen is a problematic short-term strategy and not yet proven for the long term. Nevertheless, there are major corporate interests innovating with different hydrogen technologies. Several leading car manufacturers are developing various prototype cars. These are either based on liquid hydrogen and cryogenics technology or they use a fuel cell engine refuelled by hydrogen energy stations. However, no models are available that are so far commercially viable.

In terms of new fuels, the petroleum-based car system is at a crossroads with various potential fuel systems lurking in the wings. Recently, it was commented that 'trillions of dollars will need to be invested to make the transition . . . once a certain path of investment is embarked upon, it will gather such momentum that it will be difficult to change direction'.[39] From this perspective, once investment has been committed it would set up a new path-dependent pattern. There is much activity and what we describe later as 'disruptive innovation' underway to find an alternative power source to fossil fuel. The outcome is uncertain and contested. It seems likely that hybrid fuel cars and electric/battery variants could be the basis of a new path-dependent system if they can interlock with the other components that we now examine. Toyota, as the world's largest car maker, apparently seeks to develop over the next couple of decades accident-proof eco-cars, powered by non-polluting engines that can clean the air around them and running on open roads that are free of congestion.[40] Overall, it is currently Japanese companies that are in the lead here, partly, it is said, because of the resources shortages in Japan itself.[41]

We turn now to the question of what materials future personal vehicles may be made of.

NEW MATERIALS

Steel is no longer an efficient material from which to produce cars. The weight to power ratio needs remodelling. Current cars weighing around 1 ton require only one-sixth of their available power in order to cruise and even less to move around the city. The result, say researchers, is similar to asking a 300 pound weightlifter to run a marathon.[42] If vehicles were a fraction of their current weight, the power system required would be dramatically different.

There are various developments in new materials that could shift to smaller, lighter, safer, more efficient and smarter cars suitable for insertion within a new system. The global car industry is heavily researching vehicle materials to reduce weight without sacrificing safety, since roads will remain some of the most dangerous places on earth. For example, the 'hypercar' developed by what we call in the next chapter 'disruptive innovators', the Lovins, uses advanced polymer composite materials.[43] Other possibilities include aluminium (now becoming more common), nanotechnology and carbon-based fibres.[44] The big advantage of carbon fibre is that it is one-fifth the weight of steel, yet just as strong and stiff, which makes it ideal in cars. Formula 1 cars are already made from carbon fibre so as to meet safety requirements. Replacing half the ferrous metals in current cars would reduce a vehicle's weight by 60 per cent and fuel consumption by 30 per cent. The resulting gains in fuel efficiency, made in part because smaller engines could be used with lighter vehicles, would reduce greenhouse gas and other emissions by 10–20 per cent. Such cars would be just as safe as today's automobiles.[45]

Another approach in design is shifting towards smaller micro-cars (rather than four-person family-sized cars). These would be suitable for crowded urban spaces or possibly in newly engineered micro-roads where only micro-cars are permitted. Current micro-cars include the Mercedes Smart Car, the Nissan Hypermini, Nice's Mega City and the G-Wiz.[46]

In response to pressures for environmental sustainability there is a shift towards cars that at least in the 'rich north' are part of a recyclable 'system'. The EU proposes recycling 85 per cent of vehicle components and converting 5 per cent into energy. According to new EU legislation, 95 per cent of vehicle components by 2015 will be recycled. This may signal a move towards 'systemic' thinking and practice in terms of industrial manufacture and materials.

Too much energy is wasted within the current car through heat dissipation from the engine, exhaust, tyres and so on. New materials are likely to reduce such heat dissipation and to recycle the heat as usable energy. Environmental materials will be of paramount importance to future infrastructures; this is likely to be headed by innovations in city design that hybridize modern nano-materials with natural, environmental materials, ethics and bio-mimicry.

More generally, the study of what is known as industrial ecology views industrial processes as needing to shift from linear systems to feedback processes. This involves 'waste' being injected as recyclable inputs in order to generate new processes. More recycled materials are also being developed to be used in road surfaces, in order to increase elasticity and reduce mixing temperatures in production, and thus keep costs down.

Overall, as shifts occur in car/road materials this could impact on a more efficient and less polluting vehicle system, including up to 40 per cent increased fuel efficiency through the introduction of hybrid cars; 10–20 per cent increased efficiency through weight reduction; 20–40 per cent increased efficiency through the use of smaller engines; up to 10 per cent increased efficiency through greater automobile aerodynamics and low-friction tyres; and up to 30 per cent increased efficiency through better maintained cars and roads, and safety/traffic management.[47]

Any development in car materials is likely to parallel developments in road materials in order to increase vehicle-to-road communications. Road surfaces in the last decade (in Europe especially) have seen greater 'wear and tear' resulting from increases in commuter traffic, rail-to-road heavy haulage, increased on-demand food and 'just-in-time' deliveries and general road-user traffic. This has led to not only more traffic but vehicles of much heavier loads impacting upon the life span and durability of road surfaces. The rising costs of maintaining roads largely account for increasing economic complexities of traffic management. These costs are set to escalate as the time lapse between road surface repairs decreases.

Developments in traffic management efficiency could form a major part of the new system we describe here. In the UK, private contractors have been working with the

Highways Agency to develop new fibre-optic sensor systems to track and measure road usage in order to improve traffic flow. These systems are designed to integrate with the Motorway Incident Detection and Automatic Signalling (MIDAS) network, which establishes traffic flow and real-time road messages.[48] For example, one private contractor has developed a unique system for the collection and analysis of traffic information, working with UK governmental and corporate bodies.[49] They collect information from traffic offices around the UK and combine these data with their real-time 'Floating Vehicle Data' (FVD) to provide travel time forecasts and real-time traffic updates.[50] This scheme can operate an extensive road management sensoring system that incorporates not only on-the-road monitoring vehicles (FVD) but also an array of fixed sensors that include CCTV, microwave, acoustic, infra-red and electronic inductive loop magnetic fields.[51] This information is then commercially provided for road management schemes and policy projects.

A similar system is in operation in North America where state-owned vehicles – such as governmental and emergency services – carry sensoring devices that record weather information, traffic congestion and road speeds. These data are then wirelessly transmitted to the state's Condition Acquisition Reporting System (CARS) to be used for immediate traffic management.[52]

Finally, there is the re-conceptualizing of traffic flow through modernizing the traffic-light system. Researchers at the Swiss Federal Institute of Technology, Zurich (ETH Zurich) claim that traffic flows account for as much as one-third of global energy consumption and that managing traffic flow could significantly reduce lower harmful CO_2 emissions.[53] Traffic-light systems were made in the 1960s and 70s when traffic volume was lighter and are now antiquated. The lights were also centrally controlled and not programmed to adjust in real time. Researchers at ETH propose a decentralized traffic-light system that would make travel time more predictable and optimize the flow of traffic.

These latter developments are components of what is generally known as intelligent transportation systems (ITS). Fundamental to ITS are *telematics*, which includes wireless technology, vehicle tracking, navigation assistance and car-to-car communications. This general development of what we might call 'smart' vehicles will be examined in the next section.

SMART VEHICLES

Software systems are being increasingly incorporated into car design. Symbolically Ford recently teamed up with Microsoft to enable the integration of the car with the electronic gadgets carried by drivers and passengers. These gadgets will be controlled by voice enabling, amongst other things, the sending and receiving of text messages.[54] With the increased significance of software embedded within vehicles, they may in the future more resemble computers with wheels rather than cars with chips.

And the shift that we have referred to at least briefly, to a more networked car system, would rely on such smart developments, not only between the car and the road, but from vehicle to vehicle whilst mobile. Trends in pervasive computing will enable communications between cars, roads and environments. This could facilitate a major shift in how car movement is reconstituted as a networked system rather than as cars being separate 'iron cages'. We describe this as the move towards an integrated *nexus* rather than a parallel *series*. This could produce a shift from the modern divided traffic flow to what Peters terms the 'organic flow' in which all traffic participants co-exist, aided by communications regulating the system as a whole.[55] Such networked communications would enable increased information flows between driver, car, environment and traffic management systems.

Vehicles will feature adaptable learning processes that are integrated in a software-driven system that combines physical and digital elements. Computer-embedded materials/components may also be designed to interact wirelessly with informational systems. Smart-car technologies will accelerate the merging of cars into 'virtual' territories that allow them to be *intercepted* by external sources. Material updates will be provided wirelessly from manufacturer such as in-car software upgrades via car-to-dealer communications.

Researchers on the 'Dynamically Self-Configuring Automotive Systems' (DySCAS) project aim to design an intelligent car that can 'self-diagnose and ultimately self-heal its own faults, update its own computer devices and interface with a driver's mobile phone'.[56] These latest designs in autonomous safety systems comprise 'smart materials' that download their own engine management and reconfigure their performance and safety without driver interference.

Other research in ITS include Advanced Vehicle Control Systems (AVCS) that involves vehicle/road-based systems providing increased safety and/or control to the driver.[57] These have already been positioned in the car in braking, suspension and steering systems, with more sophisticated preventative and safety technologies due in the short to medium term. This could involve Lane Assist and Intelligent Speed Adaptation.[58]

Longer term collision avoidance systems are also under development. PReVENT.[59] is a European automotive industry activity, co-funded by the European Commission, that aims to develop car safety technologies such as in-vehicle systems capable of assessing both external road conditions as well as the driver's own 'state'. INTERSAFE, the largest

PReVENT sub-project, focuses on implementing in-vehicle sensors to avoid collisions at intersections. These Advanced Driver Assistance Systems (ADAS) include in-car driver-navigation assistance systems, vehicle-tracking radar systems, lane-departure systems and road-collision sensors.[60]

Similarly, Adaptive Integrated Driver-Vehicle Interface (AIDE)[61] incorporates in-vehicle information systems with environmental monitoring sensors to create a human–machine driver interface for more 'secure' driving. The European Commission's involvement on this – Advanced Driver Assistance Systems in Europe (ADASE) – aims to introduce and implement active safety systems by harmonizing and communicating active safety functions; identifying technological needs and focusing on essentials; and preparing architectures, roadmaps and standards.[62]

And it is striking that the EU transport project considers the 'Intelligent Car' as one of its three flagship initiatives.[63] The *i2010 Intelligent Car Initiative* aims to research intelligent vehicle systems that use radar detection systems, hands-free autonomous systems, 'CarTalk' inter-vehicle communication and in-vehicle emergency communication systems such as eCall.[64] Communicative network infrastructures are being designed as part of the future vision of what may eventuate as a new kind of post-car system across Europe.

Thus, present and future vehicle communication and safety technologies seek to extend the individual car unit to connect with other cars in the immediate vicinity, in car-to-car communication, forming an integrated network, a *nexus*. This takes some autonomy away from drivers so that response-reaction times can be speeded up under such automation. Each vehicle thus in part communicates its presence to other vehicles, presuming they are similarly equipped. This is partly similar to the ways that people signal their presence to others within a social context.

The 'Car 2 Car Communication Consortium' is a non-profit organization set up by several European automotive manufacturers for researching and developing road traffic safety by means of inter-vehicle communications.[65] This is another example of what we refer to in the next chapter as disruptive innovation.

Longer range communications may be supplied by orbital infrastructures in the form of satellite networks. In order to gain independence from (if compatibility with) the US military GPS system, the EU is developing the Galileo satellite radio navigation system.[66] The European consortium behind Galileo also involves China, India, Israel and the Russian Federation's GLONASS system.

Galileo is based on a constellation of thirty satellites in constant communication with ground stations in order to provide information on vehicle location, real-time navigation, speed control and potentially pay-as-you-go cost tracking. As part of a new car system, it is expected that ground networks will embed vehicle transport within broader systemic communication infrastructures. Overall, this will include short range car-to-car communications merging with cellular and radio frequency identity (RFID) transponders and interfacing with satellite and state transport data systems.[67] The Galileo system, if it works, will shift current European transportation structures into a digitized network, as well as reinforcing practices of surveillance and enforcement (as discussed in chapter 7).

In terms of in-car systems, multimedia platforms and interactive communications will be designed *into* the overall driver experience. This may include personalized displays with wireless internet connections for accessing the Web and emails on the move, and for video conferencing (this may initially only be for passenger access, yet may change depending upon the degree of driver-automation). With digital wireless access such activities as online transactions, home–office–car computer synchronization and schedules/ meetings can be managed whilst moving. This has the effect of making the 'smart' automobile even more of a mobile office.[68] This will increasingly enable the use of traffic time as productive time.

Innovation is likely to lead to increased flows of personal information and communications 'on the move', with 'always on' being a required feature by most business travellers. This may further the development of vehicles connected in 'real time' to events and changes in its environment. Increasingly, the environment is being brought *into* the networked infrastructures of travel. The car of the future will be less an individual unit and more a networked object. 'Smart' vehicles may form part of a constantly communicating web of information and movement with 'driverless cars' being the final solution. The DARPA Grand Challenge is a prize competition for driverless cars, sponsored by the US's Defense Advanced Research Projects Agency (DARPA), the central research organization of the United States Department of Defense. DARPA awards cash prizes and each time the race occurs more driverless 'cars' complete it and are able to travel greater distances more safely.[69]

This development depends on sensors that are decreasing in size and cost. They are already being used in a range of applications: environmental and agricultural monitoring, personal health monitoring and embedded in mechanical components such as airbags.[70] Roads in the future are likely to be more of a 'sensory world'. The architecture of the surrounding environment may emerge to form an intelligent networked infrastructure that allows mobilities through a kind of 'coded space', as we discuss in the next section. This shift is made possible through the growth in digital technologies that may come to restrict and regulate individualized movement that so far generates 'over-consumption' of fossil fuels. Some smart reconfiguration could lead to increased capacity; greater integration between different transport modes; greater efficiency; increased safety and security; decreased environmental impact; and improved longevity. The development of such infrastructures requires networks, control systems, built-in resilience, transportation hubs/ nodes, pervasive software and regulated forms of social management.

However, issues of reduced privacy will move onto a wholly new level through developing a nexus system. This could generate what we might describe as an era of post-privacy where access through such spaces requires submitting details of personal information in order to gain access to such sensed spaces.[71] We return to these crucial surveillance issues in subsequent chapters.

DIGITIZATION

In this section, we consider some more general features of how digitization is transforming the conditions for movement as we move well into the twenty-first century. The significance of this can be seen from the well-known attempt by French engineers to develop Aramis in the 1980s. This Personal Rapid Transit system promised the advantages of the car – point to point service, no transfers and comfort – but within a public transport context.[72] This disruptive innovation in fact 'failed', but in part this may be because it was ahead of its time. It was developed before the 'digital revolution' had significantly developed. Physical transport has mostly been a matter of engineering, but in recent times it is increasingly 'smart'. And it is set to become even 'smarter' and this will affect the range of future developments.

The ULTra system commencing at Heathrow's Terminal

5 in 2008 will provide Personal Rapid Transit quite similar to the way in which Aramis had been envisaged in the 1980s. ULTra involves on-demand driverless travel using its own guideway network to take small groups of passengers to various destinations in moving pods.[73] It is unlikely that such systems could ever replace the car, but its development may be significant in a post-car future within certain prosperous, newly built cities in the rich north of the world. The potential importance of Personal Rapid Transit systems is especially advocated by Edmund Rydell in developing what he calls *The Transportation Renaissance*.[74]

In this section, we will consider the more general way that digitization is shifting vehicles from a private space to a privatized (and paid for) space. Software is already used in commerce to automate and cross-reference information databases, such as in categorizing queuing and congestion times for premium and non-premium phone-in customers.[75] Callers are categorized and 'privatized' through social-sorting software in telephone exchanges. Physical location influences the priority status of the caller and their access to various services.

And it could be argued it is only a small and 'logically rational' step towards prioritizing road use in a similar way according to location, route, travel necessity, time and financial status. What is likely to happen, as a means of dealing with traffic problems, is a new era of *social sorting* of travel through digitizing networks of road travel. These will emerge first in richer and more developed markets. Urban theorist Stephen Graham's term for this social coded space is 'software-sorted geographies' in which selective access is organized within socio-technical systems.[76] With these coded assemblages and techniques much mobility will be rendered inconvenient, if not impossible. For example, levels of road pricing may designate high demand urban corridors that are designed for specific traffic and premium road space, with access to these highly sought after routes being technologically enforced.[77]

Such 'software sorting' may be significant for creating fractured, or tiered, privatized movement beneath the seemingly smooth scapes of surface flows. In a post-car system access to road space would probably shift to becoming a priced commodity. This would be dependent on users having the technology standardized in their cars, and the resources, such as finance and flexible time, to engage with a mobile 'nexus' of individualized networked travel. Such travel and personal mobility would also need to be interconnected with databases, which in turn would provide the framework for the corporate privatization of cities, roads and cost quantified movement. It may be that a post-car system would have to be constructed around social inequalities of a 'splintered urbanism'.[78]

The concern is that the car can no longer be considered as sustainable within dense urban regions, given the increase in car users and the foreseeable increase in road congestion problems in city areas and privatized routes. The days of the car as the gateway to 'unfettered' freedoms and spontaneous 'get aways' are numbered. The sheer complexity of issues, from individual user rights, individualized pricing schemes, car security, identity validation, etc., will require complex systems of informational databases and coded spaces. We foresee that this will necessitate a move into data structures as a form of social sorting, within which different kinds of movement may be negotiated and 'permitted'.

Data structuring, based on the coding of space and the cross-referencing of information (database referencing), may regulate how movement is enacted through socio-technical systems. This will also increase the perceived need for real-time location sensing and the streaming of information, very similar to how GPS systems are currently used in cars today. This does not imply that car movement will be coerced. The sensing and regulation of traffic may soon become accepted as part of everyday 'normalized' social practices, just as traffic-lights or the regulation of drink and driving are relatively normalized.

Further, there are measures to tackle vehicle theft through remote immobilization. For example, Electronic Vehicle Identification (EVI) allows for the identity of a vehicle to be read and recorded remotely. This would provide security against uninsured, unlicensed and untaxed driving. However, once this became common it would pave the way for more draconian policies. For example, already in the UK the Association of Chief Police Officers and the insurance industry want electronic identification that extends to drivers through biometric recognition systems.[79] Such systems may involve in-vehicle biometrics that checks the driver before permitting car use, such as deterring those with high blood alcohol levels. The UK Association of Chief Police Officers and the motor industry are also in talks to develop a technology that will allow for external third parties (such as the police or rental agencies) to enforce remote immobilization of stationary vehicles in the event of criminal misuse and illegal behaviour.[80]

This development would extend current services such as General Motors 'OnStar' in-vehicle safety and security system. This provides 24-hour customer care access and immediate connection to emergency assistance in the case of an accident. GM has also announced that in 2009 they will equip all new models with an updated version of OnStar that allows police to enforce remote immobilization of the vehicle. A similar 'service' is offered by Nissan's 'CarWings' in-car software which calculates the fastest route to a given destination based on real-time traffic information. Information on the car's fuel consumption is then sent back to the 'CarWings' central website, allowing members to compare their driving performance against that of other members.

Technologies that relay information, such as sensors and road cameras, are part of the networked infrastructure that may lead to more distributed and pervasive computerized environments. One UK report foresees the following scenario:

> Automated vehicles all communicating with the smart roads and with each other and back-end services will create a completely new information environment within which intelligent infrastructures can be built.[81]

A shift towards increasingly intelligent surroundings ('ambient intelligence') is an emerging feature of pervasive, ubiquitous computing in cars and environments. And enhanced programming power may generate an embedded environment of connectivity, whereby objects, places and spaces will be invisibly – and often wirelessly – linked to an intelligent network or Web. Once the computing power and grid is in place it can be used and expanded upon at marginal cost, making intelligent infrastructure networks possible and sustainable. This ambient vision involves potentially thousands of embedded and mobile devices (or software components) interacting to support both user-centred goals and activities as well as control-centred procedures and new forms of surveillance, as we examine in chapter 7.

The complex management of transportation would be maintained through self-programmable and self-adaptive computational systems to cope with the increased information and data flows created by linking and connectivity of smart vehicles. Data will need to be processed, analysed and formatted at unprecedented levels by digital systems. Data within complex networked infrastructures will have to go beyond the stage of storage into efficient use and management. As both hardware and software will need to further develop before such scenarios can be realized, it is not enough to envision increasing information flows and digitization if there is not the practical capacity to organize and manage these flows.

CONCLUSION

Urban spaces in the rich north will increasingly become 'coded environments'. These urban environments may form part of the mesh of intelligent transport systems. Software will become as crucial to mobility as physical capacity. Urban structures will shift towards serving as data nodes that increasingly merge and share information with increasingly pervasive digital infrastructures and databases.

However, these 'intelligent networks' will exist alongside the physical architecture of existing urban spaces, just as most 'new technologies' involve additions to existing 'old' technologies.[82] The meshing of old and new technologies brings further uncertainties as to how the future will unfold.

Indeed, social practices will not be simply moulded by these new forms of digital technology and software. They will adapt and/or appropriate particular socio-technical developments in complicated ways. Systems often demonstrate unforeseen and unpredictable consequences, including the likelihood of computer crashes and system failure. Some have described the ways that systems can generate normal accidents that are predictable and regular features of the system in question.[83]

Thus, the potential shift towards embedded digital infrastructures will not be a smooth transition. Systems often react in a non-linear fashion to such changing conditions. Nothing neatly follows from the development of this digital environment. The ambient/intelligent environment will thus be a dynamic one, depending on its complex intersections with old and new forms of social organization, as we elaborate in the following chapter. None of the technologies described in this chapter will occur 'on their own' and none will automatically bring resulting organizational characteristics into being.

5

ORGANIZATIONS

[The automobile] can't be blamed for anything. Its conscience is as clear as Monsieur Citroen's conscience. It only fulfils its destiny: it is destined to wipe out the world.

Ilya Ehrenburg, *The Life of the Automobile* (London: Serpent's Tail, 1999), p. 175.

INTRODUCTION

In the previous chapter, we examined four sets of 'technological' developments that might come to be part of a post-car system. At the same time we argued against the view that new 'technology' in itself *produces* new patterns of life. This is partly because causes run in many complex and interdependent ways, as indicated in the diagram with which we commenced the previous chapter. And this is also because we should not simply separate out technology as something autonomous from the organizations and forms of social life with which it is intertwined.

So in this chapter we turn to four transformations in 'organizations' that may come to be components of a post-car system. We consider first a number of ways in which vehicles may be less privately owned and more shared and accessed collectively, developments that are growing in part through new forms of *digitized* payment. Second, we examine various transformations in policy which undermine the ever expanding building of new roads only for cars. There are many initiatives to shift to a more mixed 'mode' policy model. Third, various changes in the nature of social life to do with the location of home, work and leisure could make it less likely that car travel will continue to be as dominant as it was during the fateful twentieth century (as we saw in chapter 2). And finally, we briefly note that many of the major technological and organizational developments outlined in this and the previous chapter have been innovated by various agents 'experimenting' with a new system. And such a system is one where they do not know how it might ultimately turn out. We describe this experimentation as that of 'disruptive innovation' and note how many developments may come to be components of a future low carbon travel system. We begin this chapter by outlining various ways in which vehicles are becoming less privately owned and controlled.

DE-PRIVATIZING VEHICLES

New 'smart' technologies are already enabling people in certain rich societies to share, schedule and access cars through various systems which de-privatize cars. These include car-sharing, cooperative car clubs and smart car-hire schemes.[1] In the past few years, car-sharing has developed significantly in many countries in Northern Europe and in part in North America. It has been commercialized by a small number of mainly new innovative companies. As cities in Europe, North America and Asia face increasing residential parking problems and associated congestion, there is a significant turn to commercial and cooperative car-sharing schemes. One of the largest single companies, Mobility, has 60,000 members, 2,400 cars and offers the largest network of such stations in Switzerland (1,050).[2] Two popular US car sharing companies are Flexcar and Zipcar,[3] yet at present the US systems are less spontaneous, since customers often have to book cars in advance, similar to renting practices, rather than near real-time use.

The UK's first 'hire-by-the-hour' car club scheme named Avis CARvenience was set up in Oxford. Other car clubs in 2008 include CityCarClub, Streetcar and Whizzgo.[4] Such schemes are not restricted to urban areas. Rural areas schemes have been initiated by The Countryside Agency in order to mobilize members of rural communities whilst reducing private car use and ownership.[5] Such car clubs have been established in Cornwall, Devon, Wiltshire and West/North Yorkshire.

These car-sharing clubs usually involve smart card technology in order to book and pay, with flat monthly fees and pay-as-you-drive costing. The ease and flexibility of booking a car over the internet, as well as by mobile phone in many cases, are making these car-sharing schemes increasingly attractive. Occasionally, schemes involve the use of smart card technology in order to gain access to one's car as well as to pay for it. This development is likely to gain in importance.

Other more customized forms use the internet for searching and booking car services. In the UK there is 'Peasy – Car Parking Made Easy,' which is an online site for booking or offering car parking space. Peasy's mission statement is 'to provide a platform to enable people to travel to locations more efficiently and easily through enabling the spread of information and using underused resources'.[6] This scheme is similar to an online market-place where people can also offer their own parking spaces for others to use and enter negotiations over price based on short–medium–long-term requirements. Peasy also encourages home-owners to sign up and offer their underused driveway, garage or secure parking space for rent, thereby earning significant additional income. Such services make it easier for people to participate in distributed schemes and provide financial incentives.

A similar online service is currently offered in New York through Hitchsters, which connects travellers so they can share taxis and split the cost to and from local airports.[7] Hitchsters allows prospective taxi-sharers to look up a co-rider on an online notice board or to leave information. As soon as a share becomes available, the person is contacted by both a text message to their mobile phone as well as an email giving the first name and mobile number of the co-rider to contact. As an added security the company retains the phone numbers of all successful matches in case of disagreements. Gender specific co-riders can also be specified. The largest lift-sharing company is said to be liftshare.com with nearly a quarter of a million members in the UK.[8]

Some cities in Europe and North America have also been experimenting with bicycle ride-share schemes for local journeys as well as to facilitate movement between different forms of public transport. Cities such as Lyons, Stockholm, Munich and Portland, influenced by developments in Amsterdam, introduced bike kiosks around the city for members to pick up bikes and use them. Generally, the cycle club member pays a minimal annual fee (around 10 euros/$15) for a smart card that they swipe at a bike kiosk. Bikes are then rented for up to 2 hours at a time, with the first 30 minutes free. Users then pay for each subsequent 30 minute use. A similar scheme is soon to be introduced into areas of New York, with 100 bikes to be placed in each designated neighbourhood. In the summer of 2007, Paris massively upped the scale of this by introducing 1,450 new kiosks providing 20,000 bicycles scattered throughout Paris.[9] The Mayor of London is examining how such a scheme could work for London.

Another new service – termed 'Bicing' – was introduced in Barcelona in 2007. The 'Bicing' scheme entitles subscribed users to use any of the 1,500 available bicycles located across the city's subways and train stations.[10] This service also has a yearly membership fee and provides a smart card to enable free use for the first 30 minutes, charging 30 cents for each subsequent 30 minutes. This is used in combination with a network of city public transport that includes energy-saving trams and environmentally friendly subways. The Bicing online homepage provides real-time information on bicycle availability by station, city maps, pick-up and drop-off points, bicycle-friendly roads and membership information. In the first month, Bicing attracted over 3,000 users by providing local residents with alternative travel facilities for short-distance localized urban journeys.[11] Within a few months this figure jumped to over 30,000.

Overall, these developments reflect the general shift in contemporary societies from economies of ownership to economies of access, this being a major change in the nature of contemporary consumer societies. The economy of access is shown in the delivery of many services on the internet that now involve paying for 'downloads' and not for owning CDs or DVDs outright.[12] This shift would involve paying for 'access' to travel/mobility services rather than the outright ownership of vehicles.

One consequence of such a shift is that if vehicles are not owned, then the co-ops or corporations providing 'car services' would undertake both the short-term parking and the long-term disposal of the vehicles once they are no longer functioning. The former would significantly reduce the scale of car parking needed, since vehicles would be more 'on the road', while the latter radically improves recycling rates. This would facilitate recycling a high proportion of components from vehicles that are 'dead'.

Overall, then, with improved digital management and security it is possible for a major shift in the nature of cars, from being 'owned' and driven by private individuals, to de-privatized vehicles owned by cooperatives or corporations and then 'leased', parked and recycled. The spreading of the notion of 'access' via the routine practices of the internet may help to facilitate this major shift in contemporary economies with potentially important consequences for future transport and travel patterns.

NEW TRANSPORT POLICIES

Indeed, such a shift would connect to and be part of the shifting in transport policies which is proceeding on a world scale. Restructuring movement is high on many policy agendas and would be crucial in developing a post-car system. In particular, there is already a noticeable move away from 'predict and provide' policy models, especially in Europe and parts of Asia. This 'predict and provide' model involved analyses based upon predicting increased travel by road especially because of increased incomes, and then providing for that increase by building new roads.[13] And those new roads then enabled the prediction to be realized in a self-fulfilling fashion. Much of the road building bonanza in the last few decades of the twentieth century stem from widespread acceptance and implementation of 'predict and provide'.

However, it is something of a global trend in the last decade or two for public bodies to develop alternative mobility scenarios to this 'predict and provide' model. Such public bodies and many NGOs advocate what have been called 'new realist' policies. These involve integrated public transport, better facilities for cyclists and pedestrians, advanced traffic management, better use of land-use planning, real-time information systems and a wider understanding of how transport impacts on both local and global environments.

This critique of 'predict and provide' is well seen in a

report produced for the UK Department for Transport in 2005.[14] This made the following recommendations for improving residential travel and reducing car use, congestion, air pollution and accidents. Suggestions included improving accessibility and travel choice for reaching local facilities; improving public transport provision for people in nearby developments; increasing scope for child-friendly housing layouts with fewer roads, vehicle movements and parking areas; complementing nearby travel plans, and possibly even assisting them in achieving more ambitious initiatives; improving access by the wider community to the residential development by sustainable modes of transport; representing good practice and providing an educational tool to help change perceptions about the convenience and benefits of not using the car where alternatives are present; achieving more attractive environments that contribute to regeneration and renewal; and increasing the marketability of these developments as households are helped to change their travel behaviour away from the car.

It is also striking how transport policies in the rich north are sometimes now influenced by alternative models of transport from elsewhere. Curitiba in Brazil is one such model.[15] It involves separating traffic types and establishing exclusive bus lanes along the city's arteries. As a result, there is a safe, reliable and efficient bus service operating without the hazards and delays inherent to mixed-traffic bus services and with fewer delays to car routes. Over 1,000 buses make 12,500 trips per day, serving 1.3 million passengers. And there are five different types of buses operating in Curitiba including a new 'bi-articulated' bus on the outside high-capacity lanes. These bi-articulated buses – the largest in the world – are three buses attached by two articulations and capable of carrying 270 passengers.

Similar transport innovations continue to be under

development around the world, such as Guatemala City; Pune, India (2006); Bangkok; Santiago, Chile; and Lagos, Nigeria (2007).[16] Such developments can ease inner-city heavy traffic as car drivers use modernized and efficient bus services. London, following on from its 'successful' congestion charging scheme, is investing in a new fleet of energy-efficient buses, including several specially adapted and powered by fuel cells. Also, dense urban regions are digitizing their transport infrastructures in order to organize traffic more effectively through systems that bring about increasing transfer between different modes of travel.

Transport polices also increasingly encouraged people to shift modes by emphasizing the 'cost' to each individual of each mode.[17] Various computer-based systems qualify, quantify and calculate respective costs for car users. From car insurance to road pricing and car emissions, the road user will be subject to monitoring and individualized cost restraints and responsibilities. 'Intelligent' road usage involves educating the car driver to make 'smarter' individual choices about when to travel and how to make those journeys. Car 'performance' is likely to become more enmeshed within management systems that favour capacity, safety, security and databasing. This will entail new ways of privatizing and costing road use to support car users making 'smart' decisions as to where and when to drive.

An investigation by the UK's Highways Agency recently generated a 'Vision 2030' which suggested that within a couple of decades:

> The management of the highway transportation system in its totality will become highly automated and increasingly real-time. . . . New technologies will allow for real-time pricing of transportation facilities to increase efficiency, make better use of spare capacity, and reduce congestion delays. This will be supported by systems that dynamically

control and advise traffic on the network to maintain traffic
flow without adversely affecting the local environment.[18]

Indeed, road space allocation may lead to traffic management systems that will prioritize journeys according to those
that are essential and those thought to be non-essential.
However, such rationing schemes will be bitterly resisted by
campaigners mobilizing 'freedom to drive when you want
where you want' discourses.

An early indicator of some aspects of these policies is how
car insurance is moving towards 'pay-as-you-drive' schemes.
This was in place by 2006 in the UK (Norwich Union).[19] Cars
are fitted with a GPS data box that gathers information on
mileage, time of travel, speed, location and direction. From
this information the customer is billed for their insurance.
Police authorities hope these technologies will be widely
used as the data stored in the vehicles can provide important
evidence in the event of accidents. This type of individualized costing is intended to encourage behavioural change
through financial incentives to drive more slowly, drive in
less dangerous and congested areas, drive at safer times and
so on. Factors behind the push for such 'behavioural change'
include public campaigning around environmental and security issues. Policies may also be increasingly introduced to
regulate social practices of mobility through increasing separation between roads and types of road users, sometimes
referred to as 'splintering urbanism' between different classes
of user.[20]

And where new roads are being built, public policy
increasingly insists that they should be networked with other
modes of travel and routes. This can be seen in the EU's *The
Trans-European Transport Networks* (TEN-T). By 2020, there
should be a transport network that much more effectively
facilitates shifting between various modes. It will consist

of not only 89,500 km of roads but 94,000 km of railways
(including 20,000 km high-speed rail lines), an inland water-
way system of 11,250 km, 210 inland ports, 294 seaports and
66 airports.[21]

So in many ways we can see a range of policy developments that break with the previous single policy of predicting
and providing roads for cars. We will see some further examples in the next chapter of wide-ranging prototype schemes
in which the car's centrality is coming to be displaced. In the
following section, we examine changing patterns of how and
where people live, work and play.

NEW LIVING/WORK/LEISURE PRACTICES

Part of a new 'post-car' policy is the encouragement of
people gaining better access to each other through living in
more densely organized places rather than having to travel
a long way to gain access. People, it is thought, should live
in denser, much more integrated urban areas that maximize
each other's co-presence. This would in effect 'coerce' people
into meeting up with people who live nearby. Access would
be improved but physical movement would be reduced.

Various studies and reports have argued for such increased
density of living as a way of reducing both car use and
long distance travel more generally. Thus, a Stockholm
Environment Institute Report recommends urbanscapes that
encourage closer proximity between places of home, work,
shops and leisure activities. This would reduce car dependence while strengthening community.[22] This call for closer
physical proximity mirrors the 'compact city' proposal of
architect Richard Rogers. The creation of the 'compact city'
rejects the dominance of the car and recommends the design
of cities in which communities could thrive at the same time
that movement would increase in volume but not distance.[23]

Proximity in this model involves increased mobility without the dominance of the car. The 'compact city' promotes living and working in higher density places so that there is an increase in the proximities of co-presence with other city dwellers, at the same time as there is less need to make individual car journeys or long-distance journeys by high speed train or air.

Rogers' ideas have been developed as 'principles of intelligent urbanism'. This theory aims to integrate various environmental, technological, sociocultural and mobility needs into urban design. As put forward by architect Christopher Charles Benninger, the axioms of such principles work towards maximizing human interaction, mobility and engagement within an environment of sustainable resources.[24]

In the UK Foresight Programme, there are recommendations for changing housing layouts to shift car use; educational tools to educate car users; and making sustainable practices more profitable for the users, with induced benefits. One scenario that describes more localized and integrated mobile patterns of travel and communications is labelled the 'good intentions' future for the year 2055.[25]

So what is the evidence that these various reports and proposals for denser living are reflecting current and future patterns of how people are beginning to live their lives? First, there has been a significant development of apartment living in the centre of rich cities in the north and of the growth of dense shanty towns in the poor south. Both these very different developments involve increased density of living and potentially lower levels of car ownership and use, especially for day-to-day journeys.

Second, there is some evidence that more people in more places do now work at home and that this is reducing some business and commuting travel. However, although virtual travel may replace some aspects of work travel, it will not replace the need for social interactions with work colleagues.[26] Nor will there easily be any reduction in intermittently visiting family and friends, even if they are living at a distance.

Moreover, each new generation tends to get a particular pattern of life established which is then path-dependent. What we might term the EasyJet generation in the rich north of the world is not easily going to accept the notion that friends should be chosen from among those near at hand, that workmates should only be viewed on computer screens, and if one's family is at a distance then it too should also only be met virtually and not physically. Or to put it the other way round, in order that local places *are* sufficiently attractive and the focus for non-car-based sociability, they have to offer an array of facilities, meeting places and atmosphere that all social groups find especially appealing. And where people do maintain connections at a distance, the types of virtual travel will need to simulate at least some of the qualities of meeting people face to face.

Third, with regard to where people go shopping there are various tendencies pulling in different directions. At least in the case of food shopping, there is an increased focus on 'local' suppliers and deliveries, including in much of the rich north of the world the significance of farmers' markets. Then there are very large distribution centres for all the major retailers with much travel to out-of-town stores. And finally, there are increases in home deliveries from these central distribution warehouses such as Amazon. A report on the UK home shopping market from the Department for Transport expects rapid growth of internet shopping.[27] If delivery vehicles were to directly substitute for car trips, then the kilometres saved per shopping load would be substantial. Telematics can provide improved efficiency in the ways that goods can be delivered to people's homes. Many delivery services already implement Radio Frequency Identification (RFID) devices in their products. Wal-Mart and UPS have invested to construct a supply chain of tracked goods from manufacturers to consumers. With increased efficiency in the purchasing, tracking and receiving of consumer goods, it is expected that home online shopping will be a strong area of expansion.[28] Such changes may reduce traffic along particular routes at peak times, as well as reducing the routines of social engagement.

Finally, there has been a general rise throughout the world of public awareness around climate change and a growth in the numbers of people monitoring their carbon emissions, their 'carbon footprint'. This is likely to have some effect in inducing some people to modify their long-distance travel and leisure patterns. This could result in the rich north in some growth in domestic tourism as people are encouraged to spend their leisure time closer to home. Exotic travel may in certain social groups be increasingly seen as extravagant, wasteful and ethically inappropriate.[29] There may come to be a shift towards the notion that a 'good tourist' is one who flies infrequently, who travels less and who tries to seek out 'local' rather than necessarily distant destinations. Some indication of this potential shift in values is given by over 1 million hits on Google for 'ethical tourism'. However, within much of the world long-haul leisure travel will probably still increase. This is especially so where there is a growing middle class that has previously not been able to travel to places around the world.[30]

So overall, there are changes here which may facilitate a reduction in the 'need' for travel. These may occur through home working and virtual meetings, through some increase in the density of housing, through some 'guilt' at travelling long distances, and through some reductions in travel for shopping and leisure. However, none of these on their own will generate low carbon patterns. Journalist George Monbiot dramatically puts the point as follows:

> A 90 per cent cut in carbon emissions means the end of distant foreign holidays, unless you are prepared to take a long time getting there. It means that business meetings must take place over the internet or by video conferences. It means that transcontinental journeys must be made by train . . . or coach. It means that journeys around the world must be reserved for visiting the people you love, and that they will require both slow travel and the saving up of carbon rations. It means the end of shopping trips to New York, parties in Ibiza, second homes in Tuscany and, most painfully for me, political meetings in Porto Alegre – unless you believe these activities are worth the sacrifice of the biosphere and the lives of the poor.[31]

'DISRUPTIVE' INNOVATION

In our account of the various potential components of a post-car system we have seen the significance of many innovators. These include not only large motor vehicle manufacturers, but other large and small corporations, non-governmental organizations, cooperatives, universities, software designers, science institutes, local councils and community-owned enterprises. These have been noted at many points in the previous and current chapter, in the context of both technological and organizational innovation.

These agents are developing in countless different ways 'disruptive innovation', innovation that may be engendering low carbon futures. These agents have been described in a recent UK report as a 'new wave of environmental pioneers' developing low carbon alternatives within many different contexts.[32] This important report goes on to recommend: 'In short, we need disruptive forms of innovation – cheaper, easier-to-use alternatives to existing products or services often produced by non-traditional players'. It further notes that this is not only a question of 'new technologies' but of 'wider forms of innovation, such as innovation in organizational forms and business models' as we have outlined in this chapter.[33]

It is central to the thesis of this book that there is much of this disruptive innovation taking place around the world, with many agents experimenting with new ways of powering, organizing, governing and experiencing travel and transport. This experimentation does not have a clear end-state. It is not that the agents are working towards some definitive outcome, some precise objective. And this is because innovation is taking place in many different contexts, including among so-called consumers or users. And actually this is not so new, since early automobiles in the late nineteenth century were, as we saw in chapter 2, the result of many kinds of user or disruptive innovation. Early 'consumers' of the car were 'tinkerers' and their tinkering came to alter and develop what we now call the car, both in a technical and organizational sense.[34]

And innovation writer Eric von Hippel has more generally described and advocated the 'democratization of innovation' whereby so-called 'users' of goods and services engage in much product modification and product development.[35] Users are often the innovators, although such innovation occurs through complex connections and relations with other producers and users. There is a kind of emergent innovation. And uncertain outcomes result from high levels of experimentation and enthusiasm among, as in the post-car case, many users and producers scattered across the globe. However, the term 'user' here is not exactly correct in that users are not simply users but enthusiastic experimenters, making tiny modifications to goods or services which then have the effect of delivering unpredicted, more systemic outcomes of the sort we have been imagining in this book. And changing the car system is such a complex business because it is a whole system, of diverse goods and services which contingently have been assembled into a stable system.

In the following chapters, we examine just how disruptive innovation is and could be with regard to the car system. Will some of that innovation disrupt the current car system? Is there a particular disruptive innovation that will be understood in retrospect to have 'tipped' the whole system? How are enthusiasm *and* experimentation being combined to produce multiple innovations by both producers and users that will disrupt the car system and prevent it from 'wiping out the world'?

6

MODELS

The automobile of the day-after-tomorrow will not be driven by its owner, but by itself; indeed, it may one day be a serious offence to drive an automobile on a public highway.

The automobile of the future will really live up to the first half of its name; you need merely to tell it your destination – by dialling a code, or perhaps even verbally – and it will travel there by the most efficient route, after first checking with the highway information system for blockages and traffic jams.[1]

Arthur C. Clarke, *Profiles of the Future* (2nd Rev. Ed) (London: Indigo, 2000).

INTRODUCTION

More than ever, the ways that people move in the next few decades will have huge implications for energy use, global politics, community relationships and the future of life

upon earth. As architect Bruce Mau points out: 'no transportation system is an island; it must coordinate all shared
systems for maximum effect'.[2] For the car to be a legiti-
mate, sustainable and productive vehicle of the future, it
needs to be re-configured within an 'organic' system that
integrates multiple means of travel as well as restructuring
the built environment and forms of social life. The car will
have to become a 'post-car'. Jaime Lerner, the ex-mayor
of Curitiba, Brazil, famous for its innovative bus system,
notes that in his experience the most important thing for an
urban centre is the mobility system, which he claimed was
not only a system of transport but 'the whole understanding of a city'.[3] How to change that whole understanding of a
city?

In this chapter, we examine several scenarios and case
studies that provide models of how such a life 'after the car'
could be configured. What is it to go 'beyond the car', how to
design and construct a 'post-car' future?[4] We examine these
questions by considering various prototypes and models of
such a future.

Architect/designer Moshe Safdie argues that if we are
to design a built environment that better suits emerging
needs, then it is necessary to 'join our personalized patterns of car travel with fixed, planned corridors of public
transportation so seamlessly as to create a singular system
of mobility. . . . Weaving the old and the new into a single
organism'.[5] This brief notion is amplified by George
Monbiot, probably the best current writer on the sociology of a future low carbon society. He says of such a post-car
future:

> It is not hard to see how a universal switch to hypercar tech-
> nologies or electric vehicles and a return to lower speeds and
> low standards of performance, accompanied by car-sharing,

tele-commuting, a car-free shopping scheme, better public
transport and better facilities for cyclists and walkers, could
cut emissions by more than 90 per cent.[6]

Already, various post-car mobility projects are underway
worldwide. In this book we have highlighted various processes, influences and impacts that are integrating the car *as
a system* into future mobilities. The future of the car, then,
is in transition within various different systems according to
local context. This recognizes how dense urban centres have
different mobility requirements compared with more sparse
residential and rural areas.

So we will now discuss various models of the future, both
general scenarios and specific cases on the ground, all models
which highlight the possible emergence of systems that are
'after the car'. We begin with scenarios that involve the shift
from *sprawl* to *small*.

SCENARIOS FROM SPRAWL TO SMALL

It is increasingly noted how much urban life based around
long-distance commuting is no longer able to offer much
pleasure, safety or comfort. Much car use in built-up urban
areas in the rich north, but also in those large cities in Latin
America and Southeast Asia, is characterized by 'suburban
sprawl'. Such sprawl has been described as: 'low density,
large-scale single function districts such as office parks, retail
malls, and single family housing tracts'.[7] This urban form
can be difficult to serve with public transport and generates personalized car use. This suburbia is 'best understood
as the greatest misallocation of resources in the history of
the world'.[8]

In the previous chapter, we noted various architectural
projects that are attempting to reinvent urban metropolitan

areas through notions of increased density and closer proximities. One key idea is that of smart growth, or smart
sprawl, which sees the reconstruction of urban centres into
more dense mixed-use areas encouraging a combination of
walking and public transport. The concept of 'smart sprawl'
considers how urban, residential networks are supported by
transit nodes that can provide efficient and sustainable access
to close proximity services and amenities. In this way, smart
sprawl reduces car dependence and shifts onto supporting
local suburban economies and neighbourhoods.

Similarly, urban environmentalist Herbert Girardet
describes 'smart growth' made up of housing developments dense enough to significantly reduce private car
use. According to Girardet, researchers 'found that 17
dwellings per hectare support a fairly frequent bus service, 22 support a light railway network and 37 support
an express bus service that people can reach from their
homes on foot'.[9] A dense residential zone would encourage
shared modes of travel, thus reducing individual car use.
With over half of the world's population already living in
cities, high density living is becoming the global condition.
Therefore, it is imperative that such dense urban zones are
viewed as potentially modifiable ecosystems and developed
constructively so as to improve access and to reduce long-
distance movement.

This vision of the future is similar to the 'Urban Colonies'
scenario in the UK Foresight Report 'Towards 2055'. This
involves a potential future of more compact, denser urban
centres where transport is more localized.[10] Table 6.1 below
sets out the difference between 'sprawl' and notions of a
'compact city':[11]

Table 6.1 Differences between 'sprawl' and 'compact city'

Sprawl	Compact city
Low density	High density
Zoned development	Mixed-use development
Segregation of functions for living, working, recreation	Integration of functions for living, working, recreation
Segregation of demographic and economic groups	Mixed-income communities
Car dependence	Predominance of pedestrians and cyclists
Disconnected public spaces	Interconnected walkable network of large- and small-scale public spaces
High-speed transport networks and increased road infrastructure	Minimized need for transport and planning for walking and cycling
Parking, buildings and freeways	Parks, landscaping and cycle paths
Minimum parking spaces	Parking space capping requirement
Sense of anonymity	Sense of community
US urban model	European/Asian model
Developed from about 100 years ago	Developed from about 9,000 years ago
Large scale developments	Neighbourhood/human scale developments
Superstores and big shopping complexes	Corner shops, local shopping areas, farmer's markets
Mass housing and commercial/ industrial districts	Capping of allowable space for commercial/ industrial districts.
Driven by market forces	Driven by vision and master plan
High energy	Low energy
High CO_2 emissions	Low CO_2 emissions

Smart growth involves establishing an urban network of nodes that service a public transport infrastructure connecting various suburbs and neighbourhoods. Residents will be able to walk or take mass transit, there being, in theory, a couple of choices within a short distance from home. Steffen envisions this future as improving forms of urban sociability:

> the physical, the neighborly, the visceral and urban and the virtual, the connected, the digital and networked – these are symbiants, not competitors. The public square and wifi complement each other. Public transportation and high density go extremely well with the kind of highly networked, extremely social lives which digital people live today.[12]

Several urban schemes have already implemented the 'smart places, smart growth' paradigm. This can be seen in various European cities which have established various practices to accommodate mobility within a dense urban environment and especially to shift people away from car dependence. Examples of such cities are highlighted on the UN 'Best Practices' database.[13]

Zurich has implemented several measures within the city perimeters to encourage the use of fuel-efficient cars as well as reduced daily car commuting. These measures include: training in fuel-efficient driving; promotion of fuel-efficient cars; encouragement of fuel-efficient freight transport; private parking management to reduce daily car commuting; and the combined use of concessionary public transport cards/tickets.[14] This is being expanded. New transport policies seek to guarantee a transport access point within 300 metres of places of work and residence; a maximum waiting time of 30 minutes for any public transport; the introduction of extended routes so there is reduced changing for passengers; the use of a single ticket for designated journeys; better parking facilities for both off-street vehicles and bicycles; and preferential treatment for smaller cars.[15]

Similarly, policies proposed by Dutch planners include

auto-free pedestrian zones; pedestrian and bicycle traffic-
lights; intersection modifications; one-way streets for cars,
two-way streets for bicycles; reserved bus lanes for cyclists
to use; short cuts in city centres for bikes; and priority for
bikes at crossings and intersections. Other European cities
developing elements of a post-car future are London with its
congestion charging, Stockholm with its widespread availability of ethanol, and the Vauban district of Freiburg in
Germany where half of all households will live without cars,
while those areas that do allow cars to enter will have speed
limits of 15 mph. And these 'post-car' transit policies are not
limited to European cities either.

Singapore and Hong Kong, both of which have high-
density urban development, have closely integrated their
cities around the transit system.[16] In Toronto and Portland
especially, transit-oriented development has been success-
fully implemented.[17] One example is the town of Orenco
Station lying 15 miles west of Portland, US. In 1999, it was
selected by the National Home Builders out of nearly 1,000
entries for their 'Master Planned Community of the Year'
gold award. Orenco Station is a new transit-oriented community of 1,800 homes, a town centre, office, retail and local
employment. It was designed as a neighbourhood community and organized around a pedestrian spine that extends
out towards a grid of walkable tree-lined streets and parks.
It is serviced by a light rail tram service that runs every 10
minutes throughout the area. This both discourages car
use, which is no longer essential, and promotes a walkable,
pedestrian-friendly community. Orenco Station is an example of a new town designed to contrast with the sprawl that
characterizes much of US suburban growth over the twentieth century.

However, in many larger cities in Africa, Asia and Latin
America, there are still increasing levels of car ownership

related to rising population. Yet new trends in urban mobility are growing in influence, and recently prompted the creation, in 2001, of the *Charter of the New Urbanism*. This states:

> We advocate the restructuring of public policy and development practices to support the following principles: neighborhoods should be diverse in use and population; communities should be designed for the pedestrian and transit as well as the car; cities and towns should be shaped by physically defined and universally accessible public spaces and community institutions; urban places should be framed by architecture and landscape design that celebrate local history, climate, ecology, and building practice.[18]

The movement *NewUrbanism.org*[19] was established online in 1998 and has grown to promote 'good urbanism, smart transportation, transit-oriented development and sustainability'.[20] The organization promotes policies for national and local governments to revitalize and 'densify' many existing cities and towns into walkable, mixed-use communities, with bicycles and trains as the major forms of transport.[21] Out of this 'new urbanism' movement has also emerged a trend in urban development called *transit-oriented development*, or TOD.

Transit-oriented development, as modelled at Orenco Station, involves the creation of compact, walkable communities based around forms of mass public transit in order for people to maintain their quality of life without dependence on a car for personal mobility. The TOD movement promotes itself as a 'major solution to the serious and growing problems of *peak oil* and *global warming* by creating dense, walkable communities connected to a train line that greatly reduce the need for driving and the burning of fossil fuels'.[22]

This scenario of transit-oriented development involves the following: walkable design with the pedestrian as the highest priority; the train station as a prominent feature of the town centre; regional zones with close proximity to office, residential, retail and civic uses; high-density, high-quality developments within easy reach of a train station; support transit systems including trolleys, streetcars, light rail and buses, etc.; designed to include the easy use of bicycles, scooters, etc.; reduced and managed parking inside a 10-minute walk circle around the town centre/train station. The TOD movement cites how very many benefits follow from these designs.[23]

We now highlight various case studies that involve varying elements of a sustainable post-car vision.

BREMEN, GERMANY

Bremen has been developing a transportation system that is 'integrated, clean, smart, and customer-oriented'. Elements of the urban mobility system include: multimodal hubs linking transit, cycling, car-sharing and taxis; car-sharing services and residential developments with built-in car-sharing; traffic calming to favour bicycles; bike and ride facilities; intelligent tramways; integrated smart card for transit, car-sharing, and banking; integrated central station for all modes; and one umbrella organization for all 35 transit operators in the region.[24]

Data collected by the Bremen Department for Building and Environment show that more than 60 per cent of trips in Bremen are made by environmentally friendly modes: cycling (23 per cent), public transport (17 per cent), and walking (20 per cent). The high percentage of bike users is credited to the Bremen system, which provides a central bike station (*Radstation*) located at the major interchange between public transport and bike. Thus, commuters can leave their bike on their way to work or on the way home as the *Radstation* provides 1,500 guarded storage units, as well as providing services such as bike repair, rental and washing.

Another example of Bremen's 'Intermodal Integrated Transportation' system (as they call it) are the so-called 'traffic cells'. These are a system of one-way streets which 'dis-attract cars from the area' in a bid to attract cyclists. Also, the one-way streets are two-way for cyclists, creating an inner urban 'closed system' for car users. Within this urban architecture is integrated a tram network, which the Bremen authorities consider to be the backbone of their public transport system. The tram system makes use of 'intelligent' traffic-lights that recognize when the tram is present, calculate the usual time for boarding and disembarking and then changes to allow the tram to continue as a road priority. The tram system also provides real-time information for passengers at all its stops.

In order to facilitate ease of mobility, Bremen introduced a new card that combines a bank card, electronic transit ticket, as well as being an access key to the city's car-sharing scheme. This card is called, somewhat tongue-in-cheek, the *eierlegendewollmilchsau*, a German term that means 'egg-laying-wool-milk-sow'. In other words, it denotes a 'one card fits all' strategy. The 'egg-laying-wool-milk-sow' card can be used for booking cars in the car-sharing scheme, with cars being booked in real time since the booking office is available 24 hours a day. The car-sharing operator Cambio has approximately forty stations around the city with over 2,750 customers using the service.[25] This car-share scheme has already replaced approximately 700 privately owned cars and eliminated the need for almost 700 parking spaces.[26] Part of Bremen's integrated mobility strategy is to combine car-sharing with housing developments in a bid to reduce resident parking space by one-third. This is similar to Beddington, UK (see below).

Finally, as part of Bremen's 'integrated mobility strategy' the city has erected what it calls *Mobil.punkt* stations which are combined public transit hubs that bring together car-sharing, taxis, cycling and public transit. Each *Mobil.punkt* station serves as a terminal that provides travel information, such as various taxi price calculations to the main city locations. Bremen's 'integrated mobility strategy' has been designed not to eradicate the car but to integrate its function into a more sustainable network of alternative transit options so as to reduce car dependence.

THE BEDDINGTON ZERO ENERGY DEVELOPMENT (BEDZED)

This much smaller disruptive innovation has been developed by the Peabody Trust. It is intended to be the UK's largest 'carbon neutral eco-community' and is described by its developers as 'the first of its kind in this country'.[27] The primary design concept is to create a net-zero energy environment so that renewable sources will produce as much energy as the community consumes. Further, energy from renewable sources will ensure that BedZED is a carbon neutral development, making this development environmentally sustainable, with the use of roof gardens, sunlight/solar energy and waste water recycling.

The BedZED community comprises of 82 residential homes (of mixed tenures and sizes), as well as commercial buildings, an exhibition centre and a children's nursery. As part of a move towards 'responsible urban citizenship', BedZED residents keep track of their heat and electricity use by way of meters that are fitted in each home and office, thus relying on a feedback mechanism. Also, all homes and offices are fitted with low energy lighting and energy-efficient appliances. Specific to BedZED will be a small-scale 'combined heat and power plant' (CHP), which harnesses the heat that is produced as a by-product of generating electricity and puts this to further use. The heat from the CHP, it is claimed, provides hot water for BedZED residents, with each home or office having a domestic hot water tank that doubles as a radiator for peak times. The CHP plant is powered by off-cuts from tree surgery waste, which is itself a carbon neutral fuel. It appears that on an architectural level BedZED addresses environmental, social and economic needs.

In terms of urban mobility, the developers behind BedZED have focused on realizable ways to reduce car dependency. The Peabody Trust seeks to demonstrate that car dependence can be reduced. They have introduced the first legally binding Green Transport Plan as a condition of planning permission. This plan promotes alternative means of mobility such as walking, cycling and use of public transport. Also, an onsite car club called 'ZEDcars' has been set up as a car pool to supply local residents with their personal mobility. The experimental BedZED community has been designed to encourage alternatives to car use with good local public transport links, including two railway stations, two bus routes and a tramlink. BedZED aims to reach a target of a 50 per cent reduction in fossil fuel consumption by private car use over the next 10 years.

Significantly, BedZED is the first zero-energy housing development in the UK to incorporate a car club. Yet mobility in BedZED is not just about vehicle transport; it is an integrative approach combining pedestrian needs, travel flexibility, sustainable energy practices and overall community well-being. Part of this all-round policy includes a 'pedestrian first' policy with good lighting, drop kerbs for prams and wheelchairs and a road layout that keeps vehicles to walking speed. Onsite charging points for electric cars and a free public electric vehicle charging point is already available in Sutton town centre. BedZED's 10-year target is to produce enough electricity from photovoltaic panels (which convert sunlight into energy) to power 40 electric vehicles. It is hoped that a mixture of private cars and vehicles available through the car club will minimize fossil fuel use as the community develops. For owners of electric vehicles energy and parking will be free.[28]

The integrative transport-lifestyle project that BedZED has initiated, similar in parts to the Bremen scheme, enables residents to live a more sustainable lifestyle around modern networking and mobility. In the next case study, there is more emphasis on disruptive innovation from the citizens themselves.

THE 'TRANSITION TOWNS' MOVEMENT

Examples of public participation and citizen action are to be seen in the 'Transition Towns' movement which emerged from Kinsale, this being Ireland's first 'Transition Town'. Rob Hopkins established the 'Kinsale Energy Descent Action Plan', which is considered to be one of the first attempts at designing a timetabled strategy for taking a town away from fossil fuel dependency. Later, when Hopkins moved to Totnes in Devon, UK, the 'Transition Town' network was established for citizens to form town forums to create strategies for developing low carbon energy in a 'post-peak oil' world. They describe the need to respond 'to the twin challenges of Peak Oil and Climate Change.[29] The 'Transition Town' network, in its mission statement, aims to:

> inspire, inform, support and train communities as they consider, adopt and implement a Transition Initiative. We're

building a range of materials, training courses, events, tools
and techniques, resources and a general support capability
to help these communities. . . . We're hoping that through
this work, communities across the UK will unleash their own
collective genius and embark on an imaginative and practical
range of connected initiatives, leading to a way of life that is
more resilient, more fulfilling and more equitable, and that
has dramatically lower levels of carbon emissions.[30]

The 'Transition Town' initiative provides an inspiring
model for local citizens to engage with their urban environment, including the requirement for low carbon mobility
involving increased walking, cycling, and public transport.
Since the public launch of 'Transition Towns' at the Totnes
Civic Hall, the movement has screened films in various towns
and villages, and given talks to raise awareness. One project
to come out of this has been the introduction of the 'Totnes
pounds' currency that can only be spent in local shops around
Totnes. It is hoped that this initiative will spread to other
'Transition Towns'. Representatives of the movement have
also conducted 'oil vulnerability auditing workshops' with
local businesses to see how they can reduce their reliance
on oil. Other local projects set up under the scheme include
running workshops on growing fruit and vegetables, bread
baking and sock darning.[31] The initiative also strengthens
the community and goes some way to promote car-reduced
towns/cities. So far, there are over thirty towns and cities in
England signed up to a 'Transition Town' plan, with others
in Ireland, Wales, Scotland, and as far afield as Australia and
New Zealand.[32]

However, this innovative movement is largely restricted
to smaller towns, where civic engagement and localized sustainable practices from the ground up have some chance of
success. Hopkins, who started the movement, believes that

the only way the same model can work in large cities is if they split into smaller scale sustainable neighbourhoods.

In our next case study, we change scale and examine how one massive downside to China's enormously rapid urbanization and industrialization is that pollution has become even more severe and especially destructive. And climate change is now on China's agenda.

DONGTAN, CHINA

In summer 2007, China unveiled its first national plan for dealing with climate change, declaring, though, that environmental concern should not be at the expense of economic development.[33] The 62-page report did, however, state China's aim to reduce energy use by a fifth before 2010, whilst increasing the amount of renewable energy, including more wind, nuclear and hydro power. Amidst China's rapid industrial growth and future goals the leadership stresses that it remains committed to supporting what it terms 'sustainable development and poverty eradication'.

Part of this plan entails shifting a huge number of people from rural areas into both existing and newly constructed cities. China announced that it plans to build over 400 new cities within the next 20 years, with around 300 million people expected to switch from agrarian farming to urban-industrial lifestyles.[34] The deliberate state-supported migration of millions of people into cities is unparalleled and will have massive implications for the infrastructures of work, housing, transport, energy and the environment. With such high targets for future urbanization, China is aware that not all future cities can be modelled on existing high carbon design and especially on rapidly growing sales and use of cars and lorries. Therefore, the Chinese authorities are planning to construct various eco-cities, getting as close as possible to a zero carbon city in their flagship project of Dongtan.

The plans for Dongtan are, on paper, staggering in their innovative environmental design. Dongtan is to be built on Chongming Island in the Yangtze River Delta on an area the size of Manhattan Island (86 km.²). There will be a city of three villages, to be completed in phases, with the first phase planned for hosting an initial population of roughly 10,000 by 2010, in theory in time for the World Expo in Shanghai. Within the next four to five decades, Dongtan is expected to become home for an estimated 500,000 people. Already a tunnel and bridge linking Chongming Island to Shanghai is under construction, with the intention of showcasing to both Chinese urbanites and to the outside world that an environmentally sustainable city is possible.

The owners of Chongming Island, and thus Dongtan, are the Shanghai Industrial Investment Corporation (SIIC), which has handed over the planning and design of Dongtan to Arup, the global planning, engineering and design consultancy. Arup has come up with a design for an 'eco-city' that is sensitive to its specific environmental surroundings. There is a large wetland area on the southern part of the island which is a migratory reserve for one of the rarest birds in the world – the black-faced spoonbill, a white bird with a long, flat beak. A buffer zone is planned between the city and the wetland area, with the buffer's narrowest point being 3.5 kilometres wide. This will result in only about 40 per cent of the land area of Dongtan being built on, which Arup plans to use for a city that will grow into several cities, each of which will be connected by cycle routes and public transport corridors. Residents will be able to access various parts of the city by tram, bus, bicycle or by walking. Arup aims to design a city where it will not take people more than 7 minutes to walk from any part of the city to a bus or tram stop. Central to the planning of Dongtan will be the forms of mobility within the city and proximity between various forms of transit.

For example, any cars/vehicles entering Dongtan will have to run on alternative renewable fuels (including the possibility of hydrogen), with easy access to varied modes of public transport including fuel-celled buses and solar-powered water taxis along canals and lakes. A combination of cycle paths and pedestrian routes will reduce noise and air pollution, with visitors to Dongtan parking their cars outside the city and using public transport to enter. Also, the plan is for all delivery trucks to park at 'consolidation warehouses' on the edge of Dongtan before the goods are loaded onto shared 'zero emission' delivery trucks and transported into the city. In terms of fuel Dongtan will make use of various renewable energy sources such as wind turbines, bio fuels and recycling organic material.

Further, modern innovative building technologies will be used to create buildings that can reduce energy requirements by up to 70 per cent, with green roofs being placed on buildings to improve insulation and water filtration.[35] Arup hopes that these measures will create a city of zero carbon footprint, or as close to it as is feasibly possible, with a primary focus on resource efficiency.

Dongtan's urban mobility designs – integrating public walkway corridors, canal taxis, energy-efficient public transit – is an ecosystem combining movement with hugely reduced energy. The advantage of Dongtan is that it begins as a blank slate, and thus free from many of the design imperatives built into the global cities of the nineteenth and twentieth centuries. Dongtan may become a model for sustainable urban development both in China and elsewhere. It may demonstrate that a post-car city of the sort we have been elaborating can be developed and that horizontal sprawl is not inevitable.

However, China still shows many opposing trends in energy consumption. In 2006, China burned more than twice as much coal as any other country, a consumption which amounted to 39 per cent of the global total, reinforced by China's continued strong growth in constructing new power stations.[36]

Dongtan provides some indication of what might be possible when environment, energy, economy and mobility are integrated. It is of course important that Dongtan does not become only a public relations display city, but instead a model for other potential urban 'hubs' that could develop a sustainable urban post-car mobility.

In the final case study, we examine a car-free, carbon-free, zero-waste city located – of all places – in the desert.

MASDAR, ABU DHABI

The United Arab Emirates is to begin building what it describes as the world's first sustainable city, in Abu Dhabi, designed by British architect Norman Foster. The city, to be called Masdar (meaning 'the source' in Arabic), is to be located 11 miles (17 kilometres) east-southeast of the city of Abu Dhabi, beside Abu Dhabi International Airport, at an estimated cost of $22 billion. Masdar will be constructed as a dense walled city and is intended to house 50,000 people and 1,500 businesses. It is strategically located near to Abu Dhabi's principal transport infrastructure, such as surrounding communities, as well as the centre of Abu Dhabi and the international airport, connected by a network of existing road and new rail and public transport routes. The city will have no cars and aims to be self-sufficient in renewable energy, mainly solar energy from a large photovoltaic power plant. The first stage of construction involves establishing a 60-megawatt photovoltaic power plant that will supply electricity for constructing the rest of the city.

In order to generate the energy required for the city, the walls of Masdar's buildings will be covered in photovoltaic panels capable of generating 130 megawatts. The walls along Masdar's northern edge will also be constructed to let in the breeze and to keep the sun out in summer. Architects will make use of traditional 'Gulf-style' architecture to create low energy buildings, with natural air conditioning from wind towers. Electricity will also come from photovoltaic cells integrated into rooftops and a 20-megawatt wind farm. Water for the city will be provided through a solar-powered desalination plant. It has been calculated that Masdar will need a quarter of the power required for a similar sized community, while its water needs will be 60 per cent lower.[37]

Masdar's internal transportation systems have been designed to sustain the city's micro-climate. Most roads will only be 3 metres (10 ft) wide and just 70 metres long, and streets will lead onto colonnaded squares and fountains.[38] Movement within the city will be conducted through one of three levels. On one level, there will be a light railway that will connect with external transport corridors; a second level will be reserved for pedestrians; and a third for 'personalized rapid transport pods' that will resemble driverless carriages and will run on magnetic tracks, not dissimilar to the ULTra rapid transit at Heathrow Terminal Five. In order to achieve the aim of constructing from scratch a carbon-free city, cars will be banned from Masdar. The compact nature of the shaded walkways and narrow streets will encourage walking between locations, and the personalized rapid transport system will provide for longer journeys. With a maximum distance of 200 m to the nearest transport link and amenities, Masdar aims to provide support for its 50,000 inhabitants and businesses.

According to Foster, the plan for Masdar is for it to resemble the compact nature of traditional walled cities of the past, yet it will also be fully connected to external transport and fuel corridors. The surrounding desert around Masdar will contain wind farms, photovoltaic farms, research fields and plantations, so that the city will be self-sustaining despite its exceptionally harsh environment. Further, the external plantations will supply crops for the city's biofuel factories, whilst at the same time helping to reduce waste by acting as carbon sinks to offset gases produced in the factories.

Masdar represents the creative, innovative, and financial resources to construct a new city of the twenty-first century embodying current, and future, environmental and energy concerns. All its energy needs will be provided by renewables – photovoltaics, concentrated solar power, wind, waste-to-energy and other technologies. There will be zero transport emissions within the city, with waste being diverted into composting or re-used. All waste water will be reused and drinking water will be desalinated with solar energy. Much of the building materials will also be taken from recycled or certified materials.[39]

While there are concerns that the Masdar model, like China's Dongtan, may just be a 'display city' for the oil-rich Gulf state, it more importantly demonstrates the capacity for using new materials and sustainable transport and living models going beyond any existing urban system. It builds on the ideas of the 'compact city' and of smart transportation, transit-oriented development and sustainability. In this sense, it displays a systemic thinking moving away from previous path-dependent systems. It is a peculiarly located model of the possibilities of life 'after the car'.

LIFE 'AFTER THE CAR'

So in this chapter we have outlined a variety of cases that suggest some possibilities of moving to a post-car pattern.

These cases illustrate various processes that are increasing the likelihood that at some point the present fossil fuel car system will turn out to be a fossilized system. We have seen in these cases examples of all the eight interdependent processes that we described in the previous two chapters. These changes that we described at some length included: new fuel systems, new materials, smart-cars, de-privatization, post-car transport policies, digitization, new work/living patterns and disruptive innovation. These interconnected developments show that much more than the car matters. As architect Bruce Mau puts it, 'When everything is connected to everything else, for better or worse, everything matters'.[40]

Also of significance is that connections between physical and virtual spaces will be further enhanced. In this context, it is worth noting the recent phenomenon of virtual online worlds. Second Life is the most popular manifestation of an alternate realm for enacting 'meetingness' and social interaction. Second Life was launched in 2003 by web developer Linden Research, Inc.[41] and at the end of March 2008 approximately 13 million accounts were registered (although a large percentage of these are inactive). Statistics published by Linden Research show that in January 2008 residents spent 28,274,505 hours in the user-defined world, interacting, networking, doing business, or other activities such as going for a stroll.[42] It is interesting to note that regular users/participants in Second Life create an avatar, refer to themselves as 'residents', and feel that they have a stake in the upkeep of the online community. This participatory involvement is strengthened by giving residents intellectual property rights over their own digital creations which they are able to buy, sell and trade with other residents.[43] Commerce in Second Life is handled by the 'Linden dollar' (now a trademark), and there are currency exchanges where residents can exchange real world currencies for the 'Linden dollar' (L$).[44] A number of online residents in Second Life are now able to provide for their primary source of income through virtual transactions.[45]

Already a significant commercial and corporate presence has emerged in such online worlds as Second Life, with many powerful businesses and educational establishments vying for visibility. Corporate and military recruitment is also taking place on Second Life as well as security operations to track terrorists.[46] Speakers at the 2008 Virtual Worlds conference in New York announced that there are now more online avatars than there are actual people in the US.[47] Increasing convergences between physical and virtual worlds may be utterly significant in future decades, presuming, that is, that technological infrastructures are not severely disrupted. Virtual worlds are able to offer a place for social meetings and engagements, business meetings/transactions and other forms of mobility, without in a literal sense leaving one's chair.

Although we are not positing virtual online worlds such as Second Life as a post-car case study, it does offer a scenario of how online communities could form part of a nexus contributing to the design and patterning of a 'post-car', 'post-physical mobility' future. We note that in a globally networked world of increasing interdependencies, the future of cars, cities, personal mobility and the conditions of life are fearsomely interwoven. The future of the car is partly the future of human life.

In the final chapter, we discuss some alternative futures of potential post-car worlds, alternatives that we have so far only alluded to. We will show that the combination of processes outlined in chapter 1 that derive from the fateful twentieth century, of global heating, the peaking of oil, virtual worlds and of massive cities, make likely some bleak futures for social life in general.

7

SCENARIOS

INTRODUCTION

In this book, we examined how four major processes are impacting on the future of travel and transport. They are changing the climate within which mass mechanized movement is and will take place. These processes are the possibly rapid heating of the earth and its many global consequences, the peaking of oil supplies, the increased digitization of many aspects of economic and social life, and the development of massive ungovernable and unequal cities through global population increases. In chapter 1, we established the empirical significance of each of these and something of their likely trajectory over the next few decades. We noted that the increased digitization of life provided major opportunities as well as huge risks in moving to low carbon futures.

And these processes collectively undermine the continuation of the high carbon societies of the twentieth century. Their development almost certainly means that such high carbon forms of life cannot continue; there will be an ending to the carbon hubris that has been the overwhelming legacy of the last century. But of course that 'ending' is uneven, uncertain and unpredictable. But it is likely that components of that ending will occur sooner rather than later and in poorer places first but with many effects elsewhere. But because these are 'global' risks to high carbon economies and societies, so their consequences will not be reducible to specific places but will seep out across much of the globe.

And one very significant element of the twentieth century is certainly due for transformation. In the high carbon hubris of the twentieth century, the car system was particularly iconic. We described the century of the car in chapter 2 and showed how its tentacles crept into the orifices of property, power and prestige around the world. The car and its friends remade life and have provided the current century with awesome challenges. How can mass movement be sustained without the carbon supplies that are its lifeblood? What might replace or substitute for the car? What might be after the car?

In chapter 3, we briefly indicated how those questions might be examined, that is, by considering the car as a path-dependent system locked in since the late nineteenth century. This system has specific characteristics that enable it to adapt and evolve, becoming central to, and locked in with, the leading economic sectors and social patterns of twentieth-century capitalism. This system as a way of life, an entire culture, promotes and colonizes the notion of convenience rather than simply speed. It has redefined movement, pleasure and emotion in the contemporary world, transforming the fitness landscape for other mobility systems that have to find their place within a landscape formed and maintained by this car system.

But in chapters 4 and 5, we examined whether this system might just come to change. We examined a large set of interdependent processes that swirl around, potentially changing the car system and its environment. The processes that we examined ranged from the technological to the organizational, economic, policy contexts and social patterns. We maintained that technological determinism is not the right model here. The developments of biofuels or of hydrogen will not on their own produce a new post-car system. But at the same time change does not result only if *all* processes are somehow transformed.

So figuring out how change takes place is not at all simple. We argued that the car system is, in the language of physics, in a state of 'self-organized criticality'. The car system is neither fully secure nor fully insecure. It may get transformed like the avalanche of sand is transformed, but only because of some changes at the extreme that could tip it into an alternative system. It is, we might say, 'ripe' for tipping but that does not mean that it will be tipped. It will tip if the system has reached a 'chaos point' when the die is less cast and change is just possible through developments at the extreme. It is such extreme developments, the black swans, which can effect transformation of any such system in question.

Thus, thinking through the lens of complexity enables us to get closer to which small changes at the extreme may just provoke the equivalent of the avalanche for the current car system. And it will be this small change(s) that will mean that the car system, that currently seems so locked in and stable, may be ended like a pile of sand. In chapter 6, we examined some specific cases where the car is on the retreat or is being so reconfigured that there is movement to an 'after the car' system. In particular, these case studies bring out the importance of what we call disruptive innovation, innovation going against the grain and seeking to establish in unexpected locations in unpredicted ways low carbon futures. And in doing so, it may sediment new low carbon systems, although we will only know its true significance in a few decades' time.

In this final chapter, we go 'back to the future' and examine scenarios of mobility systems in the context of the four processes outlined in chapter 1. We argue that there are three convincing scenarios for the period around the middle of this century (or before). These scenarios we term 'local sustainability', 'regional warlordism' and 'digital networks of control'. We briefly describe them, indicating evidence that suggests that elements of each of them are already present in some places to some degree. Components of each scenario are lurking in the wings of contemporary societies.

Moreover, the three scenarios each imply a very different 'after the car' system. Each demonstrates that a high carbon 'business as usual' car system is not likely to be still with us by 2050. And how quickly the current car system is placed within the dustbin of history will in part determine which of these three scenarios is the one most likely to be widespread by the middle of the century.

What unfolds between 2010 and 2050 will not be the outcome of some pre-determined set of processes. Small changes may have big effects if they were to upset the 'self-organized criticality'. The relevant processes are reciprocal and not exclusive in their effects. There will be no smooth transition to a post-car future – there are too many uncertainties, unknown processes and future interconnections involved here. For example, 'peak oil' is not only a matter of energy supply but also of the social fabric that has been 'lubricated' by black gold from around 1900 until today. In particular, there are many positive feedback loops that take these various systems away from equilibrium. Each system, moreover, forms the environment for every other system, and so as the environment changes each system is forced to adapt.

The later sections of this chapter are concerned with outlining and assessing the three scenarios of 'local sustainability', 'regional warlordism' and 'digital networks of control'. Before that, however, we consider some of the issues of 'security' that are framing many elements of contemporary economic, social and political life. When we set out the significance of climate change, peak oil, digitization and mega-cities, we are outlining a range of 'security' issues and noting that how those issues unfold will determine the nature and significance of the different scenarios. We also briefly examine the importance of neo-liberalism and 'empires' in the emerging relations around the world. First, we turn to issues of security and insecurity that seem to have become *the* way of thinking about society and politics in the contemporary world.

SECURITY

Many argue that the twentieth century symbolically ended on September 11th, 2001 with the Hollywood style destruction of the twin towers of New York's World Trade Center (it also marked the end of the relatively peaceful post-Cold War borderless 1990s). The events of that day certainly cast a very long shadow over the early years of the new century, years characterized by massive new insecurities. And the government of the most powerful nation ever to strut the world's stage, the US, has sought to determine that it is indeed insecurity from terror that is the most significant of contemporary insecurities.

And in order to deal with that particular global insecurity, the US pronounced the need for a global war on terror, to drive out terror and terrorists, especially when they hail from Islamic countries and are owners or custodians of black gold. And that 'war' is viewed as a military war with almost no other policy or discourse seen as relevant. Partly as an effect of this strategy of overwhelming force, this war on terror has, however, done almost nothing to reduce the insecurities from such terror. Within Iraq and Afghanistan it has generated even more terrorism, unimaginable bloodshed and widespread and degrading corruption.

And just as it appeared clear that the war on terror has run into the sands (of Iraq and Afghanistan), so another war on new insecurities has come to occupy the world's centre-stage. It is also not without irony that this new war has been ignited by the US President that never was. Al Gore galvanized his troops for this new war, not with the 'shock and awe' bombing of Baghdad, but with the powerpoint slides of the movie *An Inconvenient Truth*.

And many now argue even on Capitol Hill that the powerpoint slides indicated a greater truth, that the insecurities of climate change are indeed more important than those of contemporary terrorism. There is an emerging body of argument that argues for going *beyond terror* and examining a range of post-terror threats to the global order.[1] Of course, in the Middle East the wars on terror and climate are highly interconnected through the pursuit of plentiful oil. The US's attempt to keep the 'home fires [and car engines] burning' has helped to engender Jihadist Islam.

In much of the world outside the centre of climate denial, the US, this new war on climate change is rapidly becoming the global orthodoxy.[2] The European Union sees the insecurities of climate change as a crucial domain in which it is ahead of the US, which is locked into a particular outdated path of the war on terror (until President Obama, that is).

In the UK, David King, the Government's chief scientific adviser at the time, claimed as early as 2004 that climate change is a far greater threat to the security of the world than international terrorism. While John Ashton, the Foreign Secretary's Special Representative for Climate Change, stated that 'there is every reason to believe that as the 21st century unfolds, the security story will be bound together with climate change'.[3]

We will now indicate some of the insecurities that climate change is engendering and note some connections with the peaking of oil, the digitizing of security and population growth.

Generally speaking, climate change is no longer simply an environmental issue but its effects are everywhere, transforming the conditions for a 'secure' life for almost everyone around the world.[4] In a 2008 report, the Oxford Research Group highlighted the multiple socio-economic disruptions generated by climate change.[5] Over the next decades, the three essential resources for human life will be food, water and energy. Rapid climate change, the peaking of oil and the growth in population makes all of them less 'secure' and will engender extensive refugee movement and civil unrest.[6]

Especially important will be positive feedback loops. Actions by governments imposing new forms of security upon contested peoples and regions may generate new forms of resistance. The security consequences, especially in high-density large urban centres, could be significant as a 'crunch' hits the daily lives of everyday, working people. Resistance to protective measures would lead to further resentment towards incumbent governments, leading to the possible breakdown of social order and further draconian measures of state security, which would seem to be being trialled in Shenzhen in China with 200,000 surveillance cameras.[7] There are potentially many positive feedback loops and system moves away from equilibrium.

The significance of these insecurities can be seen in the £12 million contract awarded in 2007 by the UK Ministry of Defence to the Hadley Centre in order to research which are the regions, nationally and internationally, where climate change and environmental disruption will create conflict and security threats.[8] Similar studies have been instigated by other governments, with the aim of assessing defence and security capabilities in the face of converging processes where the consequences will be local as well as international.

A recent 2007 US report on the impacts of climate change noted that 'while both the stability of the civil order and its ability to suddenly collapse are *prima facie* political occurrences, they are almost invariably precipitated by a witches' brew of causal factors, which can include climate or weather stress'.[9] There are various catastrophic insecurities that a climate change era will engender, as we now briefly outline.

First, there will be an increase in the number and scale of 'failed states' (and failed 'city states' such as New Orleans in late 2005). These states will be unable to cope with oil shortages and the droughts, heatwaves, extreme weather events, flooding, desertification and so on brought about through global heating. Their instabilities will then spread across borders, affecting neighbouring regimes through forced migrations, weakened public health and degraded conditions of life. For example, various NGOs report how climate change could within the next few decades generate up to 200 million environmental refugees.[10] What we might call 'environmental disturbances' would further exacerbate socio-political conflicts and on occasion lead to intercommunal violence and repressive responses. President Museveni of Uganda regularly refers to climate change as an act of aggression by the rich against the poor.[11] It is likely that international relations between countries will increasingly reflect many of these processes, of environmental disturbances, flows of environmental refugees and global resentment against the high carbon societies of the 'rich north'.

Second, maritime boundaries will become particularly susceptible to 're-evaluation' through climate change. In such cases, hostilities may well result, such as over new transport routes through the Northwest Passage.[12] Transport and energy supply networks rely on ports that are of course located on coasts or river deltas. Rising sea levels would bring huge disruption to these networks. Movement could grind to a halt with quite small increases in sea levels and this would seriously affect resource supplies and especially the delivery of food. And this is even true in the US. Potentially, the greatest impact on transportation systems will involve the flooding of roads, railways, transit systems and airport runways in coastal areas because of rising sea levels and surges brought on by more intense storms. They will require significant changes in planning, design, construction, operation and maintenance of transportation systems, according to a new report from the US's National Research Council.[13] And indeed, it will be those nearby coastal areas that attracted all those sun worshippers that will be the first to disappear under these rising sea levels.

Third, there will be insecurities occurring in the supply of clean water. The Secretary-General of the United Nations, Ban Ki Moon, told delegates at the first Asia-Pacific Water Summit in December 2007 that water scarcity threatens economic and social stability and is a 'potent fuel for wars and conflict'.[14] It is calculated that a temperature increase of 2.1 degrees would expose up to a staggering 3 billion people to water shortages.[15] This is partly because only 0.77 per cent of all fresh water, less than 0.007 per cent of all the water on the earth, is available for human use. And modern food production is colossally wasteful of water. It takes, for example, 1,000 tons of water to produce 1 ton of grain. So there are huge demands from growing populations for water, especially from those living in the rapidly growing mega-cities that have to buy and transport, often using carbon-based systems, their food and water from outside the city.[16]

Fourth, there are increasingly significant problems of food security with flooding, desertification and generally rising grain costs. The diversion of land to agro-fuel production has already helped to increase food prices.[17] The price of corn tortillas has doubled in Mexico since 2006, leading to large protest marches. This pattern is being repeated in many poorer countries around the world as wheat rose in price 130 per cent in a single year, partly because of biofuel diversion and partly because of growing demand from urbanization and the effects of desertification through climate change. Furthermore, much food production depends on hydrocarbon fuels in order to seed and maintain crops, to harvest and process them and then to transport them to market. As the cost of hydrocarbon production increases through shortages of oil, 'food could be priced out of the reach of the majority of our population. Hunger could become commonplace in every corner of the world, including your own neighborhood'.[18] There are also increasingly poor harvests through big increases in temperature in Australia, as well as plummeting stocks in major fishing areas.

And yet at the same time there are more extensive food miles. A Swedish study found that the food miles involved in a typical breakfast (apple, bread, butter, cheese, coffee, cream, orange juice, sugar) equalled the circumference of the Earth.[19] And by the end of the twentieth century almost 93 per cent of fresh produce in the US was moved by truck.[20] As one food activist recently stated, 'we need to redesign our society, aiming for decentralization and localization'.[21] And of course the peaking of oil supplies and restricted food security may, in fact, forcibly bring about such localization.

So far in this analysis, we have said rather little about the overall context of the global political economy within which climate change policies are being developed. This we will now examine, beginning with neo-liberalism.

NEO-LIBERALISM AND THE AMERICAN EMPIRE

The doctrine of neo-liberalism dramatically spread out from its birthplace in the Economics Department at the University of Chicago.[22] Through the extraordinary influence of the 'Chicago boys', it has had enormous impacts over the past two to three decades. Neo-liberalism asserts the power and importance of private entrepreneurship, private property rights, the freeing of markets and the freeing of trade. It involves deregulating such private activities and companies, the privatization of previously 'state' or 'collective' services, the undermining of the collective powers of workers and providing the conditions for the private sector to find ever new sources of profitable activity. Neo-liberalism seeks to minimize the role of the state, both because it is presumed that states will always be inferior to markets in 'guessing' what is necessary to do and because states are thought to be easily corruptible by private interest groups. It is presumed that the market is 'natural' and will move to equilibrium if only unnatural forces or elements do not get in the way.

However, states are often central to eliminating these 'unnatural' forces, to destroying many pre-existing sets of rules, regulations and forms of life that are seen as slowing down economic growth and constraining the private sector. And sometimes that destruction is exercised through violence and attacks upon democratic procedures, as with Augusto Pinochet's first neo-liberal experiment in Chile in 1973. Neo-liberalism elevates market exchanges over and above all other sets of connections between people. It believes that the 'market' is the source of value and virtue. Any deficiencies in the market are the result of imperfections of that market.

And on many occasions the freedom of the market is brought about through what its architect Milton Friedman termed 'shock treatment'. And it is the state that often gets used to wipe the slate clean and to impose sweeping free market solutions. These have been found from 1973 onwards in Latin America, Reagan's US, Thatcher's Britain, post-communist Russia and eastern Europe, 'communist' China, post-apartheid South Africa and much of the rest of the world. The state is central to what global analyst Naomi Klein terms the rise of 'disaster capitalism' including the use of warfare in Iraq to force through massive compulsory privatization in its aftermath. She also describes how the disaster of Hurricane Katrina in 2005 provided the conditions for the large-scale privatization of the New Orleans school system.[23]

Economic geographer David Harvey in *A Brief History of Neo-Liberalism* describes these neo-liberal processes as involving 'accumulation by dispossession'.[24] Peasants are thrown off their land, collective property rights are made private, indigenous rights are stolen and turned into private opportunities, rents are extracted from patents, general knowledge is turned into intellectual 'property', there is biopiracy, the state forces itself to hive off its own collective activities, trade unions are smashed and financial instruments and flows redistribute income and rights away from productive activities.

This neo-liberalism has become the dominant global orthodoxy. It is articulated and acted upon within most corporations, many universities, most state bodies and especially international organizations such as the World Trade Organization, World Bank and the International Monetary Fund. David Harvey summarizes how neo-liberalism is 'incorporated into the common-sense way many of us interpret, live in, and understand the world'.[25]

And of course it has very significant implications for how climate change and peak oil are to be engaged with at the global level. Neo-liberalism promotes the notion that only markets and the private sector should develop solutions to what economists term the 'external diseconomies of economic growth'. Some neo-liberals simply expect the market to develop the solution without needing extra measures or state encouragement of any sort. The recent growth in biofuels is a good example of the kind of market solution favoured by neo-liberals to the peaking of oil and its dramatically rising price, and the growing scale of greenhouse emissions. It is probable that for a further period neo-liberalism will continue to set economic and political agendas and make widespread concerted state actions to deal with climate change unlikely.

But this is not certain, only probable. It could turn out that climate change and peak oil turn out to be issues of such significance that through some catastrophic events they lead to the dramatic modification or rejection of neo-liberalism. After all as economist Nicholas Stern writes, 'Climate change . . . is the greatest and widest-ranging market failure'.[26] Climate change shows that the private pursuit of individual gain around the world, especially since 1990, has resulted in a collective outcome at the global level which undermines the future of capitalism. This is reflected in the quote from Karl Polanyi at the beginning of this chapter. The private market seems to be destroying the very conditions of the market economy. There is an emergent contradiction at the heart of contemporary capitalism and unfolding catastrophes might just tip economic and political discourse and practice away from neo-liberal orthodoxy.

It is interesting to note that the leading economist before Friedman was John Maynard Keynes. He was famous for his advocacy of state actions in order to remedy market failure and this gave rise to Keynesianism and much of the collaborative international institutions in the immediate post-Second World War period, especially the 1944 Bretton Woods Agreements. It is worth speculating on what he would have recommended for dealing with global climate change.

Keynes also declared (in 1936) that 'p[P]ractical men . . . are usually the slaves of some defunct economist. Madmen in authority . . . are distilling their frenzy from some academic scribbler of a few years back'.[27] Milton Friedman has been that economist since the 1970s to whom 'madmen in authority' have been enslaved. But it is possible that certain very visible and mediatized climate change consequences could yet make him seem 'defunct' (Friedman died in 2006 but his ideas live on through many disciples). The possible development of a post-neo-liberal economics would seriously improve the conditions under which innovative and wide-ranging climate change policies and politics could develop across the world within the next two or three decades. Nicholas Stern's *The Economics of Climate Change* is an attempt in that direction, seeking to bring about a new post-neo-liberal consensus. His Report concludes with the post-neo-liberal rallying cry: 'reducing the risk of climate change requires collective action . . . It requires a partnership between public and private sectors, working with civil society and with individuals'.[28]

There is another reason why neo-liberalism may not

survive for ever and that stems from the possible demise of the American empire. Part of the strength of neo-liberalism has been how, in the latter years of the twentieth century, an 'American empire' remade much of the world in a neo-liberal image.[29] The ideas of neo-liberalism moved out from the University of Chicago and into a colossal range of governments and international organizations. It helped to remake economic and political relations around the world. Such an empire enabled American companies to dominate many world markets and especially emergent markets. So-called freedom often turned out to be the freedom of American companies to dispossess and then to take over industries, regions and whole countries.

But some now argue that the 'American empire' is in decline, by comparison with the European Union, China and in different ways, Islam. In the following aspects the US is no longer dominant. First, the rest of the world does not need to seek the US's protection in relation to what was the USSR during the Cold War. Second, the US's lack of oil and gas means that it is reliant on a vast and expensive scale upon unstable and unreliable alternative and often distant sources. Third, a range of evidence suggests that it has failed to maintain such a degree of scientific and technological leadership over the rest of the world and in particular Europe, Japan and China. Fourth, the US has been highly isolated because of its refusal to sign up to the Kyoto Protocol on dealing with climate change. Fifth, there have been its catastrophic failures of militarism and 'free market fundamentalism' in Iraq and Afghanistan, with these wars costing trillions of dollars. Sixth, there is the growth of the EU such that its economy and society are now larger that the US and in some ways it possesses the world's strongest currency (in early 2008). Seventh, the rapidity of China's growth means that economically it will soon overtake the US. Finally, the US continues to generate huge budget and balance of payments deficits and extraordinary levels of indebtedness and financial turmoil and insecurity.[30] The US is by no means still the undisputed world leader.

And this makes future projections of the state of global economy and politics even harder to figure out. The weakness of post-Iraq USA may provide a chaos point that opens up opportunities for many different kinds of global players. These will range from national states to non-affiliated NGOs to those employing terrorist tactics. Many of these forces will contest territory and resources, raising the status of oil–gas rich nations such as Russia and Iran. Political instability, both in the Middle East as well as in parts of Asia and Africa, would become critical, probably leading to socio-economic disruptions on an escalating scale. Such conflicts could in turn preclude global unified action against climate change, thereby further exacerbating global heating and climatic-related natural disasters as well as food and water shortages.

Alternatively, there could be increasing influence of the EU and its pursuit of a more social democratic 'European Dream'. Rifkin describes the slow death of the American Dream and argues that it is gradually being replaced by the European Dream that is, by comparison, 'more expansive and systemic in nature and, therefore, more bound to the welfare of the planet'.[31] Of the three blocs, the US, EU and China, the EU easily leads the race to develop and implement major climate change policy initiatives and innovations.

FUTURES

We turn now to the three scenarios that we consider possible in 2050. Imagining the future is not something that social scientists have been very good at and they are often criticized for trying to do so. Marx's failure to predict where and when socialist revolution would occur within capitalism led to much criticism of such attempts to predict and to bring about a particular future. Such efforts are often characterized as overly utopian. In some ways, then, futures have been left to futurologists and in this book we have considered some formulations from such futurologists (such as the recently deceased Arthur C. Clarke).

However, the awesome issue of climate change has in a way come to legitimize all sorts of institutions thinking out alternative futures. Thinking the future simply cannot be avoided. The physical sciences are now centrally involved in modelling climate futures, both technically and in more qualitative ways, and over very varied lengths of time. Sociologists Barbara Adam and Chris Groves have recently analysed how the future can be told, predicted, thought about, fought over, tamed, transformed, traded through new financial instruments, and tended especially through ideas of sustainability.[32] Much of the world's politics increasingly involves conflicts over contested futures. In this book, we are participants in this contesting of futures, in seeking to enact certain futures through developing particular kinds of analyses and not others.

Moreover, there are techniques of thinking about the future developed by various experts in scenario building and backcasting.[33] These involve first setting out a particular scenario for a future year in the light of known trends and so-called drivers of change. These are often many in number and can lead in contradictory directions.

Second, there is establishing the events and processes that would have to happen and when, in order that a particular scenario should be realized by a particular time. This will involve imagining the interdependent effects of such events and processes on each other in the future and hence on likely overall outcomes.

Third, the scenario builder will then try to determine the probabilities of those events and processes happening. This is of course beset with uncertainty, in particular because of the role in history played by what we have discussed from time to time, namely so-called black swans. These have the effect that 'we do not know what we will know'.[34] If such events are more likely to happen, then that makes plausible the scenario in question and certain policy lessons can be drawn so as to bring about that particular future.

Fourth, if the first scenario is not plausible, then this process is conducted for other scenarios and assessments. As a result, it can be determined which of the different futures seems most likely to happen or at least those least unlikely to occur.

It is also important to distinguish between three kinds of future, possible, probable and preferable futures. And the last of these, preferable futures, are often neither probable nor even possible. Moreover, even preferable futures are likely to involve both winners and losers. And achieving one set of goals almost certainly means not achieving other goals. So there are always very complex choices, even if it is possible to establish what system is preferable at a general level and even how that may be best realized.

The three scenarios developed in this chapter are drawn from a Foresight Programme prepared for the UK Government using scenario building specialists.[35] This established four travel and transport futures that were made possible through various digital and informational innovations of the sort considered in chapter 4. We have, however, modified these scenarios and developed three. We will set them out in a fairly general way, but it must be noted that future patterns will unfold in very uneven ways across the globe. All three scenarios capture this unevenness through their focus on increased economic and social variation between local areas. This pattern stems from how climate change is highly uneven in its current and likely impacts, as various analyses detail.[36] And this heightened unevenness also stems from how much of the world has been economically and politically subjected to 'neo-liberalism' and its increased inequalities.

LOCAL SUSTAINABILITY

First, then, there is what many environmentalists argue for, namely a worldwide reconfiguration of economy and society around 'local sustainability'. This sustainability or Schumacher model would involve in the words of one major report 'eco-communalism'. This envisions a network of self-reliant (and probably also semi-isolated) communities in which people live, work and mostly recreate. This eco-communalism 'could emerge from a New Sustainability Paradigm world if a powerful consensus arose for localism, diversity, and autonomy. . .Eco-communalism might emerge in the recovery from "breakdown". Under conditions of reduced population and a rupture in modern institutions, a network of societies, guided by a "small-is-beautiful" philosophy conceivably could arise'.[37]

This would involve some dramatic global shifts towards lifestyles that are much more intensely local and smaller in scale. Friends would have to be chosen from neighbouring streets, families would not move away at times of new household composition, work would be found nearby, education would be sought only in local schools and colleges, the seasons would determine which and when foodstuffs were consumed, and most goods and services would be simpler and produced nearby. There would have to be extensive building of such new local 'communes' to facilitate such localism. Planners, politicians and citizens would need to collaborate in the redesign of urban and rural centres, neighbourhoods and mobility systems focused on local access and high level facilities.[38] Long-distance travel would be uncommon.

This may be in part a response to decreased availability of cheap energy and increased global contestation. For example, an economic meltdown triggered by the collapse of the US economy may generate a kind of global push to local sustainability. This is what David Harvey argues as a likely scenario for such a 'space of hope'.[39] Alternatively, such a shift towards a local sustainability paradigm could result from climate change/environmental disruptions and social conflict. If these geo-social disruptions are critical, this could produce increasing social disenchantment against privileged consumerist and especially mobile lifestyles.

Certainly, there are already plenty of examples worldwide of NGO activity which contests the unlimited powers of capital to make and remake the world in particular as one only fit for ever expanding consumption.[40] Thus, values of community and eco-responsibility could come to be viewed as more valued than those of consumerism, competition and individualism.

This 'contraction' in human affairs would open up opportunities for more revitalized and cooperative community-based social relations. As one analyst recently predicted: 'the twenty-first century will be much more about staying put than about going to other places'.[41] In an extreme post-peak oil scenario, the use of a car may become a luxury that creates resentment amongst those unable to drive because of oil shortages. This could lead to cars being vandalized or drivers being subject to physical abuse. James Kunstler, who develops this particular scenario, believes that the future will be one of a comprehensive downscaling, downsizing, re-localizing, and the radical reorganization of lifestyle in the rich north. In particular, he states:

Anyway one might imagine it, the transportation picture in the mid-twenty-first century will be very different from the fiesta of mobility we have enjoyed for the past fifty years. It will be characterized by austerity and a return to smaller scales of operation in virtually every respect of travel and transport. It will compel us to make the most of our immediate environments.[42]

Resource depletion fears, population expansion and accelerated climate change could impact not only on future mobilities but also on social order more generally. David Harvey, in a parallel scenario, sees an ideal future society as having slowed down and become much quieter. He sees transportation becoming free and slow and this would further reinforce a globalization of localness.[43]

This scenario we see as only 'possible' and not probable. It requires huge reversals of almost all the systems of the twentieth century, as well as declining population. There would have to be a massive restructuring of economic activities and the displacement of the global organization of economy, finance and social life. It is hard to see that the events necessary for its development will take place. If the climate change and peak oil effects are so significant, then the next scenario is more probable than local sustainability albeit a lot less preferable.

REGIONAL WARLORDISM

One scenario envisaged in the Foresight Programme is that of 'tribal trading'.[44] We rename this as tribal or 'regional warlordism'. This scenario is similar to what another report characterizes as 'barbarization' where the 'socio-ecological system veers toward worlds of sharply declining physical amenities and erosion of the social and moral underpinnings of civilization'.[45]

In this 'barbaric' climate change future, oil, gas and water shortages and intermittent wars lead to the substantial breakdown of many of the mobility, energy and communication connections that straddle the world and which were the ambivalent legacy of the twentieth century. There would be a plummeting standard of living, a re-localization of mobility patterns, an increasing emphasis upon local 'warlords' controlling recycled forms of mobility and weaponry, and relatively weak national or global forms of governance. There would be no monopoly of physical coercion in the hands of national states.

Infrastructural systems would collapse and there would be increasing separation between different regions, or 'tribes'. Systems of repair would dissolve with increasingly localized recycling of bikes, cars, trucks and phone systems. Much of the time they would not be working. Cars and trucks would rust away in the deserts or would be washed away in floods. Certain consequences of climate change may partially rectify themselves as oil and other resource use declines and overall world population may plummet.

Systems of secured long-range mobility would disappear except for the super rich. Rather like living in mediaeval times, long-distance travel would be extremely risky and probably not undertaken unless armed. The rich would travel mainly in the air in armed helicopters or light aircraft. Each warlord dominated region would potentially be at war with its neighbours, especially for control of water, oil and gas. With extensive flooding, extreme weather events and the break-up of long-distance oil and gas pipelines, these resources would be contested and defended by armed gangs. Those who could live in gated and armed encampments would do so, with the further neo-liberal privatizing of many collective functions.

This could also involve what has been termed 'Fortress

World'. One reaction to a global contraction of resources would be for richer nations to break away from poorer nations into protected enclaves. There may be increasing numbers of 'wild zones' which the rich and powerful may exit as fast as possible, if and when the oil or water no longer seem to flow. Such societies would be left to ethnic, tribal or religious warlordism, to the multitudes that from time to time re-enter safer zones as migrants or as slaves or increasingly as terrorists. In Fortress World:

the elite retreat to protected enclaves, mostly in historically rich nations, but in favoured enclaves in poor nations, as well. ... Technology is maintained in the fortresses ... Local pollution within the fortress is reduced through increased efficiency and recycling. Pollution is also exported outside the enclaves, contributing to the extreme environmental deterioration induced by the unsustainable practices of the desperately poor and by the extraction of resources for the wealthy.[46]

This scenario paints a picture of 'walled cities' similar to the mediaeval period in order to provide protection against raiders, invaders and diseases. These catastrophic effects across much of the world would be similar to those that devastated societies in the past and which may do so again in the near future according to various sources.[47]

And there are foretastes of this scenario today, including the very many gated communities that have appeared around the world. One massive 'fortress' now being constructed is Moscow's *Crystal Island* designed by Norman Foster as the world's biggest building. It will consist of 27 million square feet, a 'city within a building' with 900 apartments, 3,000 hotel rooms, an international school for 500 students, cinemas, sports complexes and a 16,500 space underground parking lot. Saudi Arabia is likewise currently building various fortresses, the King Abdullah Economic City; the Knowledge Economic City; and the Prince Abdulaziz bin Mousaed Economic City, to house 5 million.[48]

Such fortresses are to guard against or accommodate massive migration from failed states and/or regions. Visions of such fortress worlds can be seen in Robert Silverberg's 1971 novel *The World Inside* set in 2381. People no longer live in cities but in massive 3-kilometre-high towers called 'urban monads' (not dissimilar to the mega-city structures proposed by Buckminster Fuller). These urban monads (Urbmons) are 1,000-floor skyscrapers arranged in 'constellations', and each 'urbmon' is divided into twenty-five self-contained 'cities' of forty floors each, with each building holding approximately 800,000 people.

More generally, September 2005 New Orleans captures what this scenario might be like for a major city in the rich but highly unequal 'north'.[49] Hurricane Katrina showed the extraordinary inequalities within disasters, with predominantly middle class whites able to flee in advance because of their ownership of cars, contacts and communications, while the poor were left both to the hurricane, but especially to the weak resources of the federal, state and city authorities. It was only the TV pictures taken from low flying helicopters that demonstrated to the world that was watching just what happens to those living in large areas of a major city when an extreme weather event washes away the resources of the poor.

Life in parts of the 'south' already shows signs of transformation through global climate change. Contemporary Afghanistan, Iraq and Somalia demonstrate many elements of this scenario and hence generate millions of refugees. Bangladesh in the low lying Ganges is the country worst affected by global climate change and yet produces tiny levels of carbon emissions. These emerging global relationships have been termed 'climatic genocide', with millions being forced to migrate away from global climate change risks so far mainly experienced in the poor 'south'.[50] Life in the 'rich north' would also turn nasty, brutish and 'shorter', as foretold in the 1982 dystopic nightmare *Mad Max 2*.[51]

Naomi Klein argues that adherents to the shock doctrine hold that crises are not necessarily bad. She notes that 'only a great rupture – a flood, a war, a terrorist attack – can generate the kind of vast, clean canvases they crave. It is these malleable moments . . . that these artists of the real plunge in their hands and begin their work of remaking the world'.[52] And that remaking can often be undertaken through dispossessing people's democratic and other rights. So we should not presume that global forces will find features of climate change unattractive, since it could provide the clean slate, the right kind of shock in order to create the Orwellian networks of control that we outline as the third scenario.

DIGITAL NETWORKS OF CONTROL

This scenario is developed from the 'good intentions' scenario set out in the UK Foresight Report.[53] This scenario involves inserting and combining digitized information *within* systems of movement, as we elaborated in chapters 4 and 5. And as such, it may bring about something that has not happened for a 100 years, a major change in the form of ground transportation. As we have seen, we may be close to a tipping point when personal vehicles are combined with a 'smart' infrastructure to develop an integrated network rather than a series of separate vehicles. This would represent a major shift as cars are reconstituted as a system rather than as the separate 'iron cages' which they have been for the past century or so.

This model would thus involve overcoming the separation

of different transport systems and replacing it with what philosopher of movement Peter Peters terms an 'organic' model. He clarifies:

> Whereas the modern style attempted to solve the problem of intersecting speeds by preventing them from meeting in the first place, the organic design style seeks to *integrate* traffic participants. In this approach, the traffic landscape had to be designed in such a way that differences in speed were minimized.[54]

Such an organic model represents a return to the form of traffic landscape found before the car system took over and monopolized most roads and which forced other road users to seek protection within separate zones (pavements, cycle tracks, pedestrianized zones).

This organic digital system, commencing in some societies in the rich 'north', would consist of multiple, dense forms of movement of small, ultra-light, smart, probably battery or hydrogen-based, deprivatized 'vehicles'. Flexibilized travelling would involve accessing such small, light mobile pods as and when required. Electronic regulators embedded in lamp-posts and in vehicles would regulate access, organize price and control the vehicle speed. Some such vehicles would be driverless. The movement of vehicles would be electronically and physically integrated with other forms of mobility. One future scenario describes the 'personal multimodal pod in which passengers can stay in comfort throughout a journey leaving all the hassle of switching between different transport modes and network levels to the pod'.[55]

It is organic because there is a mixed flow of those slow-moving micro-cars, as well as bikes, hybrid vehicles, pedestrians and mass transport. These are integrated into networks of physical *and* virtual access. There would be electronic coordination between motorized and non-motorized transport, and between those 'on the move' in many different ways. 'Smart cards' would control access to and pay for people's use of the various forms of mobility. And software systems will 'intelligently' work out the best means of doing tasks, meeting up or getting to some place or event. This scenario would not involve returning to the dominance of publicly owned, managed and timetabled buses, trains, coaches and ships. That public mobility model has been lost because of the car system that necessitates the individual flexibility, comfort and security of personal vehicles. For us this model involves the integration through information, payment systems and physical access between personal vehicles and so-called public transport.

And at the same time, neighbourhoods will need to be redesigned so as to foster 'access by proximity' through denser living patterns and integrated land use. People will live in denser, much more integrated urban areas that maximize co-presence. Such redesign would 'force' people to bump into each other, since their networks will overlap and there will be many 'meeting places' for different groups of citizens.

This scenario would involve carbon allowances as the new currency to be allocated, monitored and individually measured, so dramatically constraining much physical mobility. Where physical movement does occur, this would be subject to rationing through price or need or some kind of quota. It is clear that air travel would need to be the most heavily rationed of the forms of transport that have so far become commonplace.[56]

Much of the time physical travel would be replaced by modes of virtual access. These forms of virtual access will need to have been much developed so that they effectively simulate many of the features of physical co-presence with other people. The development of tele-immersion environments may be the start of a set of technologies that do indeed begin to simulate the pleasures and especially the complexities of face-to-face interactions.

Overall, this scenario relies upon various emergent and deeply problematic technologies: CCTV cameras; data mining software; biometric security; integrated digital databases; the embedding of digital processing within the environment and moving vehicles; Radio Frequency Identity (RFID) implants to track objects and people; automated software systems for allocating road space; smart code space to determine the route, price, access and speed of vehicles; sensors and processors to enable vehicles to self-navigate; and the likely tracking and tracing of each person's carbon allowances and carbon expenditures.[57]

So we have set out a scenario that would seriously constrain the opportunities for physical movement, and through its capacity to reduce carbon emissions from travel it is preferable to regional warlordism with regard to lowering carbon emissions on a potentially extensive scale. Components of this system are in place and we view this as a distinctly possible future scenario. However, if we backcast from 2050 there are some major complexities involved in this 'digital networks of control' scenario.

First, developing this scenario is, as noted in chapters 4 and 5, unpredictable. The tipping point should not be read off from linear changes in existing firms, industries, practices and economies. Just as the internet and the mobile phone came from 'nowhere', so if there is a tipping point here it will emerge unpredictably. It will probably develop from a set of technologies or firms or governments that are not currently at the centre of the transport industry. And this is because, according to heterodox economist Eric Beinhocker, companies do not so much innovate but it is markets that bring forth innovation.[58] The economy is driven more by the entry and exit of firms, by their emergent effects, than by individual companies that are able to adapt and evolve. It is most likely that the post-car system will first emerge in a small society or city-state where there is very dense informational traffic and with innovating market relations and culture. We need then to spot where such disruptive innovation may emerge.

Second, such an infrastructure would be very costly to implement, although it seems that much of the 'hard technology' will be in place over the next few years. Thus, the costs at a time of increasing resource constraints because of climate change may make it globally impractical to implement on an extensive scale, even if some prototype cities were able to develop such a model (such as city-states like Singapore). It is a 'first world' solution, although even here the difficulties of getting it to work are substantial. And it would require utterly massive sums to develop such a system in the emerging megacities of the poor south. Huge investment by private companies and large amounts of 'aid' from the rich north to the poor south would be necessary.

Third, these digital developments are highly intrusive and further threaten civil liberties.[59] They transform the nature of the individual person. Already many states are seeking to integrate different databases that contain 'private' information on each person. This further extension would link that information with data on each person's movement by personal vehicle and in due course by public transport. This would seriously limit the 'freedom' to walk, drive or move without record and without connections being made with other information held about that person. People and their movement become recorded and classified. However, 'smart solutions' will be contested in the name of 'freedom' especially within 'democratic' societies and where there is little 'trust' in the state. This contestation, at a time of many other conflicts around security and population management, will make such a scenario bitterly fought over.

But of course threats from climate change may become so palpable that there seems to be no alternative other than implementing systems of this sort. The shock of climate change may tip societies into these kinds of digital networks and a post-car future. And anyway, such freedoms have already been seriously curtailed with the worldwide 'securitization' of people's lives. Under the sway of post September 11th, and amidst an orchestrated 'war on terror,' many intrusive technologies are being rapidly introduced. The UK Government's Information Commissioner states that people in Britain already live in a surveillance society.[60]

But if this is so, perhaps people will conclude that such surveillance should be used for the purposes of 'defeating' climate change and will not necessarily contest the introduction of such a system. And even if they contest such surveillance, it may well be that that contestation will be more or less unsuccessful, as climate change provides the context for yet another version of 'disaster capitalism'.

THE FUTURE OF THE 'CAR'

In this short book we have focused on the car 'system' and what might happen to it within the next few decades. We have argued that there are three possible scenarios for 2050, each of which indicates a different post-car future. In the first, local sustainability, there is the partial replacement of the current car system with a very wide range of local forms of transport and movement. Long-distance movement is uncommon because of oil and resource shortages. Many forms of life are locally centred and concentrated. Because much movement is local, feet, the bike and many new low carbon forms of transport are to be found alongside more motorized forms. This is *post-oil localism*.

In the second, regional warlordism scenario there is the implosion of mobility. Movement is hard to achieve because of the breakdown of many of the long-range systems of mobility and communications. And travel is dangerous if one leaves behind the safety of one's particular fortress. Cars remain but they are mainly rusting versions from previous decades. Enormous efforts and skills are deployed to keep these wrecks moving and to stop them being commandeered. Few new methods of movement are to be found. We can describe this as a *post-mobility* pattern and in some ways the use and reuse of cars in some developing societies indicate the kind of improvisational, tinkering car culture that is most likely to develop.[61]

And third, there is the scenario we termed 'digital networks of control'. Here, there is a fully functioning post-car system which transforms very many kinds of vehicles away from being separate and autonomous towards the automation of movement. Digital and physical movement are integrated to form a *digital nexus system* but this is a future which will augment the integration of databases that will have direct implications for human freedom.

So it is a limited set of choices that confronts societies in the early years of the twenty-first century. And the reason for this constrained set of alternatives is, we argue, the twentieth century. That century of unprecedented energy production and consumption paid little attention to future generations. It ignored the observation made near the beginning of the previous century by Edmund Burke when he said that a society is a 'partnership not only between those who are living, but between those who are living, those who are dead, and those who are to be born'.[62] Yet many of those who are yet to be born as part of 'future generations' will be born into highly circumscribed futures. Decisions being made now are having effects upon future generations and yet those generations have no voice over those processes (unlike some agricultural societies with their notions of 'stewardship' for subsequent generations).

A series of path-dependent systems have thus been set in motion that are having their impact today. 'Regional warlordism' involves almost unimaginable reductions in the nature of economic, social and political life in the rich north. Yet moving to the digital 'networks of control' model is beset with enormous difficulties, especially cost, the problems of implementation on a worldwide scale, and likely opposition on grounds of curbing the 'freedom to drive' and threats to the 'freedom of the individual' resulting from its Orwellian character.

Moreover, the next couple of decades – a crucial period for combating climate change – are likely to be globally shaped by further system developments that are going to make the environment for moving to a nexus vehicle model even more troublesome. In particular, the 'war on terror' is already producing heightened suspicion and lack of trust in states and in their draconian securitization of populations. Within the context provided by these system developments, it may make it increasingly difficult to move to a nexus model. In this respect, the global war on terror may be 'won', but only by losing the global war on climate change.

Yet it might be possible to avoid regional warlordism if many transformations occur that bring about a tipping point in favour of digital networks of control. In this scenario, the future of *human* life may well depend on moving across a tipping point to the 'digitization' of each self and the integration of multiple databases (what China calls the 'Golden Shield'). Such a system of tracking and tracing will involve noticeable changes to the very fabric of social life, freedom of movement and lifestyles. This bargain involves a digital 'Orwellian-ization' of self and society, with more or less no movement without digital tracing and tracking, with no-one legally beyond or outside the control of digital networks (with London's congestion charging.[63] or Singapore's Electronic

Road Pricing as indicative first steps). This may tame the car system (and other energy systems) if many developments take place simultaneously, including the tracking and tracing of each person's carbon allowance which could come to function as a public measure of worth and status.

So life as such would still go on and co-presence through travel would be still achievable for many. But this is only because each individual self is tracked and traced, enabling the car system (and many other resource-hungry systems would change in parallel ways) to tip into a nexus, organic post-car system. And achieving that shift would require exceptional political leadership worldwide to ensure that personal rights are significantly protected. So far, there is no sign that states recognize the sheer economic, social and political complexities of implementing a future that would dramatically slow down the rate of carbon emissions, without huge reductions in personal freedom. And with large private sector corporations devising new 'security products', there are many reasons why a securitized future is most likely. States in an era of neo-liberalism are of course hugely beholden to the oil and other corporate interests that were routinely favoured in twentieth-century struggles.

But if it were the case that neo-liberalism was to be on a slippery slope, and if climate change became a matter of democratic politics and not just the opportunity for new corporate investment, then it is just possible to avoid both regional warlordism and digital networks. That leaves the third scenario here, local sustainability, a pattern of economic and social life that would involve the reversal of most 'advances' that the last two centuries promoted since Edmund Burke's social contract model put future generations centre-stage. This would involve a post-car model, indeed a post-oil localism. How to get from here to there in a few decades and how to ensure that many billions of people can survive through such a localism and the collapse of the international division of labour that localism would entail are massive issues. Although localism may be preferable to the other scenarios it seems less probable.

We have thus tried to indicate that the future of the 'car' is not a small question and issue. It is central to the future trajectories of economies, societies and life in the twenty-first century. Small decisions and disruptive innovations occurring now may be laying down a set of huge path-dependent patterns. These will have untold consequences for later generations, whose range of opportunities will be constrained as the peaking of oil and the consequences of climate change will have further speeded up. How the issue of personal mobility is dealt with will in part determine whether and how people live their lives down the line, in small-scale localism, in a Hobbesian war of all against all, or in Orwellian systems of digital surveillance. The twentieth century's free lunch has resulted, after a decade of global optimism in the 1990s, in some hugely bleak dilemmas for the twenty-first century. There are, we might suggest, no good outcomes after the car. It and its high carbon friends would seem to have done their best to leave little standing even as they themselves may disappear from view.

NOTES

Chapter 1 Changing Climates

1 See P. Gilroy (2000) 'Driving while black', in D. Miller (ed.) *Car Cultures*. Oxford: Berg; and see chapter 2 below.

2 See Al Gore's movie *An Inconvenient Truth* released in 2006. Also, the global warming disaster movie *The Day After Tomorrow*, released in 2004, has been one of the highest grossing films.

3 See http://observer.guardian.co.uk/international/story/0,6903,1153513,00.html (accessed 12/02/2007).

4 Two crucial major reports are N. Stern's (2007) *The Economics of Climate Change. The Stern Review*. Cambridge: Cambridge University Press; and IPCC (2007) http://www.ipcc.ch. Recent influential popular science accounts included J. Lovelock (2006) *The Revenge of Gaia*. London: Allen Lane; G. Monbiot (2006) *Heat. How to Stop the Planet Burning*. London: Allen Lane; M. Lynas (2007) *Six Degrees. Our Future on a Hotter Planet*.

London: Fourth Estate; F. Pearce (2007) *With Speed and Violence. Why Scientists fear Tipping Points in Climate Change*. Boston: Beacon Press; E. Kolbert (2007) *Field Notes from a Catastrophe. A Frontline Report on Climate Change*. London: Bloomsbury; and E. Linden (2007) *Winds of Change. Climate, Weather and the Destruction of Civilizations*. New York: Simon and Schuster.

5 For the IPCC home website go to http:/www.ipcc.ch.

6 F. Pearce (2007) *The Last Generation: How Nature Will Take Her Revenge for Climate Change*. London: Transworld.

7 J. Lovelock (2006) *The Revenge of Gaia*. London: Allen Lane (p. 35).

8 J. Hansen (2007) 'Scientific reticence and sea level rise', *Environmental Research Letters*, 2: 1–6.

9 F. Pearce (2007) *With Speed and Violence. Why Scientists fear Tipping Points in Climate Change*. Boston: Beacon Press (p. 21). For a more technical analysis, see J. Rial and others (2004) 'Nonlinearities, feedbacks and critical thresholds within the Earth's climate system', *Climate Change*, 65: 11–38.

10 See N. Stern (2007) *The Economics of Climate Change. The Stern Review*. Cambridge: Cambridge University Press, (p. 3). And see the effects of potential temperature rises in M. Lynas (2007) *Six Degrees. Our Future on a Hotter Planet*. London: Fourth Estate.

11 See http://www.abi.org.uk (accessed 23/11/07).

12 T. Flannery (2007) *The Weather Makers: Our Changing Climate and What it Means for Life on Earth*. London: Penguin (p. 235).

13 F. Pearce (2007) *The Last Generation: How Nature Will Take Her Revenge for Climate Change*. London: Transworld.

14 N. Stern (2007) *The Economics of Climate Change*.

The Stern Review. Cambridge: Cambridge University Press.

15 As well as the levels of CO_2 and greenhouses gases, other possible contributions to climate change include the periodic variations in the sun's radiation and cyclic sunspot activity, variations in the earth's orbit and spin, volcanic geothermal activity, the complex changes present within the earth's troposphere and stratosphere, and atmospheric impacts upon ocean heating and currents. See T. Flannery (2007) *The Weather Makers: Our Changing Climate and What it Means for Life on Earth*. London: Penguin. Fred Pearce notes that recent changes in climate change cannot be explained by sunspot activity since it has been declining since 1980; see (2007) *With Speed and Violence. Why Scientists fear Tipping Points in Climate Change*. Boston: Beacon Press (p. 14).

16 J. Kunstler (2006) *The Long Emergency: Surviving the Converging Catastrophes of the 21st Century*. London: Atlantic Books (p. 148).

17 See N. Stern (2007) *The Economics of Climate Change. The Stern Review*. Cambridge: Cambridge University Press, Part IV.

18 The English version came out in 1992. U. Beck (1986) *Risikogesellschaft. Auf dem Weg in eine andere Moderne*. Munich: Suhrkamp.

19 Quoted in F. Pearce (2007) *With Speed and Violence. Why Scientists fear Tipping Points in Climate Change*. Boston: Beacon Press (p. xxiv).

20 J. Lovelock (2006) *The Revenge of Gaia: Why the Earth Is Fighting Back – And How We Can Still Save Humanity*. London: Allen Lane.

21 See A. Giddens (1990) *The Consequences of Modernity*. Cambridge: Polity.

22 A well-known oral aphorism from Buckminster Fuller.

23 N. Stern (2007) *The Economics of Climate Change. The Stern Review*. Cambridge: Cambridge University Press (p. 197).

24 See J. Urry (2007) *Mobilities*. Cambridge: Polity (chapter 1).

25 Steer Davies Gleave (2006) *Driving Up Carbon Dioxide Emissions From Road Transport: An Analysis of Current Government Projections*. A Report for Transport 2000.

26 E. Black (2006) *Internal Combustion: How Corporations and Governments Addicted the World to Oil and Derailed the Alternatives*. New York: St Martin's Press (p. 262).

27 J. DeCicco and F. Fung (2006) *Global Warming on the Road*. Canada: Environmental Defense (p. iv).

28 World Wildlife Fund for Nature (2008) *Plugged In: The End of the Oil Age*. Brussels: WWF European Policy Office (p. 2).

29 G. Orwell (2000) *1984*. Harmondsworth: Penguin.

30 See http://www.guardian.co.uk/environment/2008/mar/10/climatechange.eu (assessed 13/04/08); the 2004 movie *The Day After Tomorrow* directed by Roland Emmerich; S. Hall (2007) *The Carhullan Army*. London: Faber and Faber.

31 See R. Hickman and D. Banister (2006) *Towards a 60% Reduction in UK Transport Carbon Dioxide Emissions: A Scenario Building and Backcasting Approach*. London: University College, London. http://www.vibat.org/publications/pdf/eceee_paper.pdf (accessed 31/03/08). Similar future scenarios are World Wildlife Fund for Nature (2008) *Plugged In: The End of the Oil Age*. Brussels: WWF European Policy Office, and J. Tiffin and C. Kissling (2007) *Transport Communications*. London: Kogan Page.

32 See the analysis of this high carbon US, D. Nye (1999) *Consuming Power*. Cambridge, Massachuselts: MIT Press,

which brings out the complex interconnections of auto-mobility and electricity.

33 See   http://news.bbc.co.uk/1/hi/sci/tech/3143798.stm (accessed 23/11/07).

34 E. Laszlo (2006) *The Chaos Point: The World at the Crossroads*. London: Piatkus Books.

35 For their website see http://www.ucsusa.org (accessed 09/12/07).

36 T. Homer-Dixon (2006) *The Upside of Down: Catastrophe, Creativity, and the Renewal of Civilization*. New York: Island Press (p. 1).

37 See N. Gilman, D. Randall and P. Schwartz (2007) 'Impacts of climate change: a system vulnerability approach to consider the potential impacts to 2050 of a mid-upper greenhouse gas emissions scenario', *Global Business Network*: January (pp. 1–24).

38 See http://www.peakoil.com. For a parallel analysis of 'peak gas', see J. Darley (2004) *High Noon for Natural Gas*. Vermont: Chelsea Green.

39 In 1956 M. King Hubbert, a geologist for Shell Oil, pre-dicted that the peaking of US oil production would occur around 1965–1970 (actual peak was 1970). This became known as the Hubbert curve and Hubbert peak theory (or peak oil).

40 This is the view of Colin Campbell of the Association for the Study of Peak Oil and Gas (ASPO).

41 This is the view of Kenneth S. Deffeyes as predicted in Deffeyes, K.S. (2005) *Beyond Oil – the View from Hubbert's Peak*. New York: Hill and Wang.

42 J. Leggett (2005) *Half Gone. Oil, Gas, Hot Air and Global Energy Crisis*. London: Portobello Books.

43 R. Heinberg (2005) *The Party's Over: Oil, War and the Fate of Industrial Society*. New York: Clearview Books. See J. Leggett (2005) *Half Gone. Oil, Gas, Hot Air and*

Global Energy Crisis. London: Portobello Books, chapter 2 on how to prospect for oil, and the diagram on p. 57.

44 A. Chrisafis and G. Keeley (2008) 'Oil prices: Europe threatened with summer of discontent over rising cost of fuel', *The Guardian*, June 10th, http://www.guardian.co.uk/business/2008/jun/10/oil.france   (accessed 12/06/08).

45 R. Lovett (2007) 'Russia plants underwater flag, claims arctic seafloor', *National Geographic News*, August 3rd 2007, http://news.nationalgeographic.com/news/08/070802-russia-pole.html (accessed 12/10/07).

46 http://www.guardian.co.uk/world/2008/mar/10/eu.climatechange (accessed 13/04/08).

47 O. Bowcott (2007) 'Britain to claim more than 1m sq km of Antarctica', *The Guardian*, October 17th 2007, http://www.guardian.co.uk/news/2007/oct/17/antarctica.sciencenews?gusrc=rss&feed=networkfront (accessed 18/10/07).

48 J. H. Kunstler (2006) *The Long Emergency: Surviving the Converging Catastrophes of the 21st Century*. London: Atlantic Books (p. 84).

49 J. H. Kunstler (2006) *The Long Emergency: Surviving the Converging Catastrophes of the 21st Century*. London: Atlantic Books (p. 65).

50 P. Pinchon (2006) *Future Energy Sources for Transport: Background*. Brussels: Future Energy Sources for Transport.

51 J. Leggett (2005) *Half Gone. Oil, Gas, Hot Air and Global Energy Crisis*. London: Portobello Books (pp. 12, 15).

52 'The Oil Famine Bugaboo' in *Horseless Age 2*, no. 3, January 1897, cited in E. Black (2006) *Internal Combustion: How Corporations and Governments Addicted the World to Oil and Derailed the Alternatives*. New York: St. Martin's Press (p. 66).

53 See http://news.bbc.co.uk/1/hi/sci/tech/6247199.stm (accessed 18/10/07).

54 See N. Thrift and S. French (2002) 'The automatic production of space', *Transactions of the Institute of British Geographers New Series*, 27: 309–35.

55 M. Castells (ed.) (2004) *The Network Society*. Cheltenham: Edward Elgar.

56 M. Castells (2004) 'Informationalism, networks, and the network society: a theoretical blueprint', in M. Castells (ed.) *The Network Society*. Cheltenham: Edward Elgar (p. 7).

57 G. Noble (2004) *Bin Laden in the Suburbs. Criminalising the Arab Other*. Sydney: Sydney Institute of Criminology.

58 BBC Online (2006) 'Heathrow begins biometric trials', http://news.bbc.co.uk1/hi/uk/6211122.stm (accessed 6/12/06).

59 See current European Commission funded research project known as Op-Tag – http://www.optag/consortium.com (accessed 06/02/07).

60 See WhiteHouse (2003) *The National Strategy for Physical Protection of Critical Infrastructures and Key Assets*. National Infrastructure Advisory Council (NIAC): February 2003 (pp. 1–96).

61 As seen in the recent European Space Agency projects – http://www.esa.int/esaTE/SEMKN89L6VE_index_0.html (accessed 16/02/07).

62 G. Gallopin, P. Raskin and R. Swart (1997) *Branch Points: Global Scenarios and Human Choice*. Stockholm: Stockholm Environment Institute – Global Scenario Group (pp. 1–47).

63 http://www.un.org/esa/population/publications/WUP2005/2005wup.htm (accessed 11/04/07).

64 http://www.un.org/esa/population/publications/WUP2005/2005WUP_FS1.pdf (accessed 11/04/07).

65 A team of research scientists at North Carolina State University and the University of Georgia, working with United Nations estimates, predicted that the world will be 51.3 per cent urban by 2010, with May 23rd 2007 being the 'transition day' based on the average daily rural urban population increases from 2005 to 2010. On that day a predicted global urban population of 3,303,992,253 will exceed 3,303,866,404 rural people – see http://news.ncsu.edu/releases/2007/may/104.html (accessed 24/05/07).

66 United Nations (*2006*) *Global Trends: Refugees, Asylum-seekers, Returnees, Internally Displaced and Stateless Persons Report*, June 2007 (revised 16th July 2007).

67 See on climate change and global inequality, J. Timmons Roberts and B. Parks (2007) *A Climate of Injustice*. Cambridge, Massachuselts: MIT Press.

68 R. Rogers (1997) *Cities for a Small Planet*. London: Faber and Faber.

69 See M. Davis (2007) *Planet of Slums*. London: Verso, on how there are probably 200,000 contemporary slums, mostly located on the edge of cities.

70 M. Davis (2007) *Planet of Slums*. London: Verso (p. 19).

71 M. Davis (2007) *Planet of Slums*. London: Verso (p. 133).

72 http://www.chinadialogue.net/article/show/single/en/297-Which-way-China- (accessed 11/04/07).

73 http://www.iht.com/articles/2007/05/30/asia/letter.php (accessed 04/06/07).

74 M. Chamon, P. Mauro and Y. Okawa (2008) 'Mass car ownership in the emerging market giants', *Economic Policy*, IMF: 243–96.

75 H. Girardet (2004) *Cities, People, Planet*. Chichester: Wiley-Academy (p. 136).

76 See http://www.tata.com/tata_motors/releases/20080110.htm (accessed 11/01/08).

77 R. Pinderhughes (2004) *Alternative Urban Futures: Planning for Sustainable Development in Cities throughout the World.* New York: Rowman and Littlefield Publishers.

78 H. Girardet (1999) *Creating Sustainable Cities.* Totnes: Green Books (p. 12).

79 J. Diamond (2005) *Collapse: How Societies Choose to Fail or Survive.* London: Allen Lane.

80 J. Tainter (1988) *The Collapse of Complex Societies.* Cambridge, New York: Cambridge University Press.

81 G. Monbiot (2006) *Heat. How to Stop the Planet Burning.* London: Allen Lane (p. 215).

Chapter 2   The Century of the Car

1 A.C. Clarke (2000) *Profiles of the Future* (2nd rev. ed.). London: Indigo (p. 33).

2 H. Williams (1991) *Autogeddon.* London: Jonathan Cape.

3 K. Schneider (2005/1971) *Autokind vs. Mankind.* Lincoln, NE: Universe.

4 Agreement about who constructed the first credited self-propelled mechanical vehicle or automobile is divided, with some saying that French inventor Nicolas-Joseph Cugnot built the first such vehicle in about 1769. Others claim that Ferdinand Verbiest, a member of a Jesuit mission in China, built the first steam-powered car around 1672. Likewise, the claim as to who designed the first 'engine' includes descriptions of compressionless engines from the seventeenth century (Christiaan Huygens), sixteenth century (Leonardo da Vinci), to the thirteenth century (Al-Jazari). However, a Swiss inventor, François Isaac de Rivaz, is generally credited as producing the first internal combustion engine fuelled by a mixture of hydrogen and oxygen, in 1806.

5 E. Black (2006) *Internal Combustion: How Corporations and Governments Addicted the World to Oil and Derailed the Alternatives*. New York: St. Martin's Press.

6 In the US George Selden filed a patent in 1879 based on a combustion engine on four wheels, yet delayed the granting of his patent for many years by not constructing a model of his motor car.

7 See J.P. Bardou, J.J. Chanaron, P. Fridenson and J. Laux (1982) *The Automobile Revolution: The Impact of an Industry*. Chapel Hill: The University of North Carolina Press.

8 For further details, see J.P. Bardou, J.J. Chanaron, P. Fridenson and J. Laux (1982) *The Automobile Revolution: The Impact of an Industry*. Chapel Hill: The University of North Carolina Press.

9 Mr Salom on 'Automobile vehicles' in *Horseless Age*, no. 6, April 1896, cited in E. Black (2006) *Internal Combustion: How Corporations and Governments Addicted the World to Oil and Derailed the Alternatives*. New York: St. Martin's Press (p. 64).

10 E. Black (2006) *Internal Combustion: How Corporations and Governments Addicted the World to Oil and Derailed the Alternatives*. New York: St. Martin's Press (p. 68).

11 See D. Miller (ed.) (2000) *Car Cultures*. Oxford: Berg (p. 7).

12 For a detailed history of the controversy surrounding the deliberate internal corporate sabotage of electric companies by shareholders, E. Black (2006) *Internal Combustion: How Corporations and Governments Addicted the World to Oil and Derailed the Alternatives*. New York: St. Martin's Press (chapter 8).

13 E. Black (2006) *Internal Combustion: How Corporations and Governments Addicted the World to Oil and Derailed the Alternatives*. New York: St. Martin's Press (pp. 64–5).

Charles Duryea, early pioneer of the combustion engine in the US, wrote in *Horseless Age* in August 1896 that: 'Humanity is accustomed to noise and that noise is a requisite rather than an objection in the perfect vehicle. . . . If the article (an automobile) does the work, the people will accept it regardless of noise, danger or manageability. The railroad train is not a silent affair, it is a pandemonium of noise compared with the old stage coach on the dirt road, but where will you find stage coaches today running in opposition to a railroad?'

14 E. Black (2006) *Internal Combustion: How Corporations and Governments Addicted the World to Oil and Derailed the Alternatives*. New York: St. Martin's Press (p. 163).

15 Fordism, at least in the US, involves a system of economic management modelled on that employed by Henry Ford that maintained that gains could be obtained by firms offering somewhat higher wages to allow the workers to purchase the very products that they themselves were producing, such as cars and other consumer goods.

16 See D. Nye (1999) *Consuming Power*. Cambridge, Massachusetts: MIT Press.

17 See W. Sachs (1992) *For Love of the Automobile*. California: University of California Press.

18 See Peter Merriman's exemplary account of the making of Britain's new 'driving space', the M1: (2007) *Driving Spaces*. Massachusetts: Blackwell.

19 As 'punishment' each company was fined $5,000 plus the court costs of $4,220.78, and each individual was ordered to pay $1 for 'his role in the conspiracy'. For an in-depth description of the conspiracy, see chapter 10 in the Black's *Internal Combustion: How Corporations and Governments Addicted the World to Oil and Derailed the Alternatives*. New York: St. Martin's Press (2006).

20 See the wonderful collection P. Wollen and J. Kerr (eds)

Autopia. Cars and Culture. London: Reaktion Books; as well as M. Featherstone, N. Thrift, J. Urry (eds) (2004) *Automobilities*. Special double issue of *Theory, Culture and Society*, 21: 1–284.

21 Tata Motors of India have produced the world's cheapest car, selling for less than £1500, providing the emerging Indian middle class with a 'people's car' – see http://www. iht.com/articles/2008/01/07/business/car.php (accessed 08/01/08).

22 See D. Miller (ed.) (2000) *Car Cultures*. Oxford: Berg.

23 M. Sheller (2004) 'Automotive emotions: feeling the car', *Theory, Culture and Society*, 21: 221–42. See G. Monbiot (2006) *Heat. How to Stop the Planet Burning*. London: Allen Lane (p. 144).

24 These cultural forms of autopia are elaborated in P. Wollen and J. Kerr (eds) (2002) *Autopia. Cars and Culture*. London: Reaktion Books.

25 P. Newman (1999) 'Transport: reducing automobile dependence'. In D. Satterthwaite (ed.) *The Earthscan Reader in Sustainable Cities*. London: Earthscan Publications Ltd. (p. 177). It should be noted that social democratic rich Sweden has a zero fatality policy for its roads.

26 B. Mau (2004) *Massive Change*. London: Phaidon Press.

27 B. Mau (2004) *Massive Change*. London: Phaidon Press.

28 See M. Featherstone 'Introduction', in M. Featherstone, N. Thrift, J. Urry (eds.) (2004) *Automobilities*, Special double issue of *Theory, Culture and Society*, 21: 1–284 (p. 19), especially on the technicalities of different fatality measurements which typically use World Health Organization data and analysis.

29 W. Sachs (1992) *For Love of the Automobile*. California: University of California Press.

30 On young people and cars, see E. Carrabine and B. Longhurst (2002) 'Consuming the car: anticipation, use

and meaning in contemporary youth culture', *Sociological Review*, 50: 181–96.

31 Cited in M. Morse (1998) *Virtualities: Television, Media Art and Cyberculture*. Indiana: Indiana University Press (p. 117).

32 W. Sachs (1992) *For Love of the Automobile*. California: University of California Press (p. 93).

33 W. Sachs (1992) *For Love of the Automobile*. California: University of California Press (p. 97).

34 M. Lacy (2007) *Security and Climate Change*. London: Routledge (p. 137 – italics in original).

35 M. Csikszentmihalyi (2002; new ed.) *Flow: The Classic Work on How to Achieve Happiness*. New York: Rider and Co. And see R. Pirsig (1974) *Zen and the Art of Motorcycle Maintenance*. London: Corgi (p. 5) when he describes how: 'Plans are deliberately indefinite, more to travel than to arrive anywhere. We are just vacationing'.

36 See the new study by S. Redshaw (2008) *In the Company of Cars*. London: Ashgate, which especially explores how young men and women keep such company rather differently.

37 M. Sheller (2004) 'Automotive emotions: feeling the car', *Theory, Culture and Society*, 21: 221–42.

38 R. Rogers (1997) *Cities for a Small Planet*. London: Faber and Faber (p. 35).

39 See the very sad book, E. Platt (2000) *Leadville*. London: Picador, which details the bleak lives experienced by those having to keep the company of cars along the A40 road in west London. More Autogedden than Autopia.

40 T. Adorno (1974) *Mimima Moralia*. London: Verso.

41 M. Safdie (1997) *The City After the Automobile: An Architect's Vision*. New York: Basic Books.

42 M. Safdie (1997) *The City After the Automobile: An Architect's Vision*. New York: Basic Books (p. 5).

43   R. Rogers (1997) *Cities for a Small Planet.* London: Faber and Faber (p. 153).

44   R. Pinderhughes (2004) *Alternative Urban Futures: Planning for Sustainable Development in Cities throughout the World.* New York: Rowman and Littlefield Publishers (p. 132).

45   See S. Walby (2009) *Globalization and Inequalities.* London: Sage, on the conflict between neo-liberal and social democratic visions of economy and society.

46   H. Girardet (2004) *Cities, People, Planet.* Chichester: Wiley-Academy (p. 136).

47   R. Pinderhughes (2004) *Alternative Urban Futures: Planning for Sustainable Development in Cities throughout the World.* New York: Rowman and Littlefield Publishers (p. 130).

48   H. Girardet (2004) *Cities, People, Planet.* Chichester: Wiley-Academy (p. 136).

49   Big Yellow Taxi, Joni Mitchell *Ladies of the Canyon,* May 1970.

50   R. Pinderhughes (2004) *Alternative Urban Futures: Planning for Sustainable Development in Cities throughout the World.* New York: Rowman and Littlefield Publishers (p. 137).

51   L. Mumford (1964/1953) *The Highway and the City.* London: Secker and Warburg.

52   L. Mumford (1964/1953) *The Highway and the City.* London: Secker and Warburg (p. 180).

Chapter 3 Systems

1   See *inter alia* A.L. Barabási (2002) *Linked. The New Science of Networks,* Cambridge, Massachusetts: Perseus; M. Buchanan (2002) *Small World. Uncovering Nature's Hidden Networks,* London: Weidenfeld Nicholson; D. Byrne (1998) *Complexity Theory and the Social Sciences.* London: Routledge; F. Capra (1996) *The Web of Life.*

London: Harper Collins; F. Capra (2002) *The Hidden Connections. A Science for Sustainable Living.* London: Harper Collins; J. Casti (1994) *Complexification.* London: Abacus; M. Gladwell (2000) *Tipping Points. How Little Things can make a Big Difference.* Boston: Little, Brown and Company; G. Nicolis and I. Prigogine (1989) *Exploring Complexity.* New York: W. H. Freeman and Company; J. Urry (2005) *Complexity*, special issue *Theory, Culture and Society*, 22: 1–274.

2   P. Ball (2004) *Critical Mass.* London: William Heinemann (p. 283). See E. Beinhocker (2006) *The Origin of Wealth.* London: Random House, for a parallel account of complexity economics (see Table 4-1 on p. 97, which contrasts complexity and traditional economics).

3   J. Gleick (1998) *Chaos: The Amazing Science of the Unpredictable.* London: Vintage.

4   S. Budiansky (1995) *Nature's Keepers.* London: Weidenfeld and Nicholson; M. Davis (2000) *Ecology of Fear.* London: Picador.

5   See P. Ball (2004) *Critical Mass.* London: William Heinemann (p. 571).

6   F. Capra (1985) *The Turning Point: Science, Society and the Rising Culture.* London: Fontana. E. Beinhocker in (2006) *The Origin of Wealth.* London: Random House, notes how mistaken it was for economists to borrow the concept of equilibrium from classical physics.

7   This is the argument developed in P. Ball (2004) *Critical Mass.* London: William Heinemann, which elaborates a 'physics of society'.

8   Cited in M. Buchanan (2002) *Nexus: Small Worlds and the Groundbreaking Science of Networks.* London: W. W. Norton (p. 207).

9   R. Jones (2004) *Soft Machines: Nanotechnology and Life.* Oxford: Oxford University Press. And see Michael

Crichton's nanonovel (2002) *Prey*. New York: Harper Collins.

10 J. Lovelock (2006) *The Revenge of Gaia*. London: Allen Lane.

11 See P. Ball (2004) *Critical Mass*. London: William Heinemann (p. 106).

12 See F. Pearce (2007) *With Speed and Violence*. Boston: Beacon Press.

13 M. Gladwell (2000) *Tipping Points. How Little Things can make a Big Difference*. Boston: Little, Brown and Company (p. 13).

14 I. Prigogine and G. Nicolis (1977) *Self-Organization in Non-Equilibrium Systems*. New York: John Wiley and Sons. See E. Beinhocker (2006) *The Origin of Wealth*. London: Random House (pp. 66–8), on the neglect of the second law in much economics.

15 I. Prigogine (1997) *The End of Certainty*. New York: The Free Press (p. 64).

16 I. Prigogine (1997) *The End of Certainty*. New York: The Free Press.

17 N. Stern (2007) *The Economics of Climate Change*. Cambridge: Cambridge University Press (p. 97).

18 I. Prigogine and I. Stengers (1984) *Order out of Chaos*. London: Fontana (pp. 140–1).

19 B. Arthur (1994) *Increasing Returns and Path Dependence in the Economy*. Ann Arbor: University of Michigan Press; M. Waldrop (1994) *Complexity*. London: Penguin; and E. Beinhocker (2006) *The Origin of Wealth*. London: Random House.

20 See M. Castells (2001) *The Internet Galaxy*. Oxford: Oxford University Press.

21 Brian Arthur, quoted in M. Waldrop (1994) *Complexity*. London: Penguin (p. 49); B. Arthur (1994) *Increasing Returns and Path Dependence in the Economy*. Ann Arbor: University of Michigan Press.

22 B. Arthur (1994) *Increasing Returns and Path Dependence in the Economy.* Ann Arbor: University of Michigan Press. For theoretical and empirical critique, S. Liebowitz and S. Margolis (1995) 'Path dependence, lock-in, and history', *The Journal of Law, Economics and Organization,* V11 N1 (pp. 205–26).

23 See chapter 2 above; and J. Motavalli (2000) *Forward Drive.* San Francisco: Sierra Club.

24 Quoted in M. Waldrop (1994) *Complexity.* London: Penguin (p. 49).

25 D. North (1990) *Institutions, Institutional Change and Economic Performance.* Cambridge: Cambridge University Press (p. 99).

26 D. North (1990) *Institutions, Institutional Change and Economic Performance.* Cambridge: Cambridge University Press (p. 104).

27 N. N. Taleb (2007) *The Black Swan.* London: Penguin. He notes that Francis Bacon and Arthur Koestler, to name but two, argued that the most important events are those that are the least predictable (pp. 166–7).

28 J. Urry (2007) *Mobilities.* Cambridge: Polity.

29 E. Laszlo (2006) *The Chaos Point.* London: Piatkus Books.

30 M. Gladwell (2000) *Tipping Points. How Little Things can make a Big Difference.* Boston: Little, Brown and Company.

31 P. Ball (2004) *Critical Mass.* London: William Heinemann (pp. 298–302).

32 P. Ball (2004) *Critical Mass.* London: William Heinemann (pp. 307–10).

Chapter 4 Technologies

1 E. Laszlo (2006) *The Chaos Point: The World at the Crossroads.* Charlottesville, VA: Hampton Roads (p. 39).

2 J. Urry (2007) *Mobilities*. Cambridge: Polity.

3 F. Geels (2006) 'Multi-level perspective on system innovation: relevance of industrial transformation', in X. Olshoorn and A. Wieczorekm (eds) *Understanding Industrial Transformation: Views from Different Disciplines.* The Netherlands: Springer (pp. 163–86), (p. 165).

4 M. Sheller (2004) 'Automotive emotions. Feeling the car', *Theory, Culture and Society*, 21: 221–42 (p. 222).

5 House of Commons (2004) *Cars of the Future: Seventeenth Report of Session 2003–04 (HC 319-I)*. House of Commons Transport Committee (pp. 1–54).

6 It is interesting to note that Rudolph Diesel originally designed his engine to be powered on peanut oil. Another recent project has seen a car powered on modified chocolate.

7 A. Mol (2007) 'Boundless biofuels? Between environmental sustainability and vulnerability'. *Sociologia Ruralis*, 47 (4): 297–315.

8 P. Pinchon (2006) *Future Energy Sources for Transport: Background*. Report for Future Energy Sources for Transport: Brussels.

9 P. Pinchon (2006) *Future Energy Sources for Transport: Background*. Report for Future Energy Sources for Transport: Brussels.

10 A. Mol (2007) 'Boundless biofuels? Between environmental sustainability and vulnerability'. *Sociologia Ruralis*, 47 (4): 297–315.

11 Worldwatch (2006) Biofuels for Transportation: Global Potential and Implications for Sustainable Agriculture and Energy in the 21st Century. Worldwatch Institution (pp. 1–38).

12 BRAC (2006) *Biofuels in the European Union: A Vision for 2030 and Beyond*. Biofuels Research Advisory Council: 14/03/2006 (pp. 1–32).

13 For an in-depth argument, A. Mol (2007) 'Boundless biofuels? Between environmental sustainability and vulnerability'. *Sociologia Ruralis*, 47 (4): 297–315.

14 A. Mol (2007) 'Boundless biofuels? Between environmental sustainability and vulnerability'. *Sociologia Ruralis*, 47 (4): 297–315.

15 See online BBC News report – http://news.bbc.co.uk/1/hi/world/americas/7065061.stm (accessed 04/11/07).

16 For more information, see http://www.biofuelwatch.org.uk/index.php (accessed 03/11/07).

17 M. Salameh (2006) *Can Biofuels Pose a Serious Challenge to Crude Oil?* Oil Market Consultancy Service Report.

18 A. Mol (2007) 'Boundless biofuels? Between environmental sustainability and vulnerability'. *Sociologia Ruralis*, 47 (4): 297–315.

19 E. Black (2006) *Internal Combustion: How Corporations and Governments Addicted the World to Oil and Derailed the Alternatives*. New York: St. Martin's Press (p. 287). Also, it should be noted that research is developing agro-fuel alternatives from bacteria, such as microbial energy conversion. Here, microbial energy technologies use micro-organisms to manufacture fuels through the breakdown of organic materials.

20 Worldwatch (2006) *Biofuels for Transportation: Global Potential and Implications for Sustainable Agriculture and Energy in the 21st Century*. Worldwatch Institution (pp. 1–38).

21 As described and advocated in R. Willis, M. Webb and J. Wilsdon (2007) *The Disrupters. Lessons for Low-carbon Innovation from the New Wave of Environmental Pioneers*. London: Nesta.

22 House of Commons (2004) *Cars of the Future: Seventeenth Report of Session 2003–04 (HC 319-I)*. House of Commons Transport Committee (pp. 1–54).

23 P. Hawken, A. Lovins and L. H. Lovins (2002) *Natural Capitalism: The Next Industrial Revolution*. London: Earthscan.

24 M. Maynard, (2008) 'Toyota will offer a plug-in hybrid by 2010', *The New York Times*, http://www.nytimes.com/2008/01/14/business/14plug.html?_r=1&oref=slogin (accessed 15/01/08).

25 A. Trafton (2006) 'MIT powers up new battery for hybrid cars' http://web.mit.edu/newsoffice/2006/battery-hybrid.html (accessed 24/10/06).

26 Seehttp://www.iht.com/articles/ap/2007/12/11/business/AS-TEC-Japan-New-Battery.php (accessed 15/01/08).

27 See 'Improving fuel cells for cars: a new method for making ultra-thin materials could lead to better fuel cells' in Technology Review – http://www.technologyreview.com/Energy/19710 (accessed 19/11/07).

28 WWF (2008) *Plugged In. The End of the Oil Age*. Brussels: WWF (March). There are similar plans in San Francisco Bay (*Guardian*, November 22nd).

29 See http://www.haaretz.com/hasen/spages/818359.html (accessed 29/01/08).

30 J. Rifkin (2003) *The Hydrogen Economy: The Creation of the Worldwide Energy Web and the Redistribution of Power on Earth*. London: Putnam.

31 It has since been revealed that the flammable outer-coating of the Zeppelin's skin was the cause of the initial explosion, not the gas.

32 E. Black (2006) *Internal Combustion: How Corporations and Governments Addicted the World to Oil and Derailed the Alternatives*. New York: St. Martin's Press.

33 House of Commons (2004) *Cars of the Future: Seventeenth Report of Session 2003–04 (HC 319-I)*. House of Commons Transport Committee (pp. 1–54).

34 T. Flannery (2007) *The Weather Makers: Our Changing*

Climate and What it Means for Life on Earth. London: Penguin.

35 T. Flannery (2007) *The Weather Makers: Our Changing Climate and What it Means for Life on Earth*. London: Penguin (p. 262).

36 Current research advocates single-walled carbon nanotubes to improve the hydrogen compression and storage problems.

37 House of Commons (2004) *Cars of the Future: Seventeenth Report of Session 2003–04 (HC 319-I)*. House of Commons Transport Committee (pp. 1–54); J. Romm (2004) *The Hype About Hydrogen: Fact and Fiction in the Race to Save the Climate*. Washington, DC: Island Press.

38 R. Heinberg (2004) *PowerDown: Options and Actions for a Post-carbon World*. London: Clairview (p. 129). For positive support of the hydrogen economy, J. Rifkin (2003) *The Hydrogen Economy: The Creation of the Worldwide Energy Web and the Redistribution of Power on Earth*. London: Polity. Craig Venter's new company 'Synthetic Genomics' aims to produce new micro-organisms to create hydrogen. This is still an unproven and ongoing technological investment.

39 T. Flannery (2007) *The Weather Makers: Our Changing Climate and What it Means for Life on Earth*. London: Penguin (p. 277).

40 D. Gow (2006) 'Ten years down the road: car giant foresees the non-polluting, accident-proof saloon', *The Guardian*, March 31st.

41 C. Caryl and A. Kashiwagi (2008) 'Get your green motor running', *Newsweek*, September 15th (pp. 36–40).

42 P. Hawken, A. Lovins and L. H. Lovins (2002) *Natural Capitalism: The Next Industrial Revolution*. London: Earthscan.

43 P. Hawken, A. Lovins and L. H. Lovins (2002) *Natural*

Capitalism: The Next Industrial Revolution. London: Earthscan.

44 US Department of Transportation (1999) *Effective Global Transportation in the Twenty-First Century: A Vision Document*. US Department of Transportation: 'One Dot' Working Group on Enabling Research

45 See http://www.sciencedaily.com/ releases/2006/03/060307084809.htm (accessed 16/03/08).

46 Innovative design concept cars are also on the drawing board – a notable example here is the MIT designed 'City Car', a stackable electric two-passenger city vehicle: see http://cities.media.mit.edu (accessed 12/05/07).

47 See http://www.biofuelwatch.org.uk/resources.php (accessed 02/12/07).

48 See http://www.e4engineering.com/Articles/296541/ More+go+with+the+flow.htm (accessed 04/03/07).

49 See http://itisholdings.com/index_flash.asp (accessed 16/01/07).

50 Floating vehicle data: 'Technology for the collection, analysis and forecasting of journey times using speed and location data directly from a sample of vehicles as an alternative to fixed roadside sensors' http://itisholdings. com/whatfvd.asp (accessed 16/01/07).

51 See http://proddev.itisholdings.com/worldcongress (accessed 16/01/07).

52 See http://news.nationalgeographic.com/news/2004/05/ 0521_040521_smartcars.html (accessed 14/01/07).

53 See http://www.ethlife.ethz.ch/archive_articles/071115- trafficflow/index_EN (accessed 19/11/07).

54 Presently dubbed 'Sync' it is expected to be rolled out as an option on all Ford models from 2009 onwards; see http://technology.guardian.co.uk/news/story/0,,1985151 95,00html?gusrc=rss&feed=20 (accessed 17/01/07).

55 P. Peters (2006) *Time, Innovation and Mobilities*. London: Routledge.

56 Online, T. (2006) 'On the road to intelligence', http://www.theengineer.co.uk/Articles/296543/On%20the%20road%20to%20intelligence.htm (accessed 11/11/06).

57 See a summary document entitled 'Overview of future trends': http://www.transportvisions.org.uk/documents/pdf/V2030-15_Overview_of_Future_Trends-24Apr02.pdf (accessed 22/10/06).

58 House of Commons (2004) *Cars of the Future: Seventeenth Report of Session 2003–04 (HC 319-I)*. House of Commons Transport Committee (pp. 1–54).

59 See http://www.prevent-ip.org (accessed 23/04/07).

60 For publications, see http://www.prevent-ip.org/en/public_documents/publications (accessed 23/04/07).

61 See http://www.aide-eu.org (accessed 23/04/07).

62 See http://www.adase2.net (accessed 25/04/07).

63 See http://europa.eu.int/information_society/eeurope/i2010/index_en.htm (accessed 25/04/07). And see http://europa.eu.int/information_society/activities/esafety/intelligent_car/index_en.htm (accessed 25/04/07).

64 EU (2006) *On the Intelligent Car Initiative: Raising Awareness of ICT for Smarter, Safer and Cleaner Vehicles*. European commission: 15.2.2006 (pp. 1–10).

65 See http://www.car-to-car.org (accessed 08/09/07).

66 See http://ec.europa.eu/dgs/energy_transport/galileo/index_en.htm (accessed 16/01/07). Galileo was due to become operational in 2008, yet is currently 3–4 years behind schedule.

67 M. Bell (2006) 'Policy issues for the future intelligent road transport infrastructure'. *IEE Proceedings. Intelligent Transport Systems*, 153 (2): 147–155.

68 See E. Laurier (2004) 'Doing office work on the motorway', *Theory, Culture and Society*, 21: 261–77.

69 See http://en.wikipedia.org/wiki/DARPA_Grand_ Challenge#2007_Urban_Challenge (accessed 20/03/08).

70 B. Sharpe and T. Hodgson (2006) *Towards a Cyber-Urban Ecology.* Foresight Project on Intelligent Infrastructure Systems (pp. 1–44). See Foresight (2006) *Trends and Drivers in Intelligent Infrastructure Systems: A Literature Review for the Foresight Project on Intelligent Infrastructure Systems.* Foresight Project on Intelligent Infrastructure Systems.

71 S. S. Network (2006) *A Report on the Surveillance Society* (for the Information Commissioner). September 2006 (pp. 1–98).

72 B. Latour (1996) *Aramis or the Love of Technology.* Cambridge, MA: Harvard University Press.

73 See http://www.atsltd.co.uk (accessed 20/03/08).

74 E. Rydell (2000) *The Transportation Renaissance.* US: Xlibris Corporation.

75 S. Graham (2005) 'Software-sorted geographies'. *Progress in Human Geography*, 29: 562–80.

76 S. Graham (2005) 'Software-sorted geographies'. *Progress in Human Geography*, 29: 562–80.

77 S. Graham (2004) 'Constructing premium network spaces: reflections on infrastructure networks and contemporary urban development', in R. Hanley (ed.) *Moving People, Goods, and Information in the 21st Century.* London: Routledge.

78 S. Graham and S. Marvin (2001) *Splintering Urbanism: Networked Infrastructures, Technological Mobilities and the Urban Condition.* London: Routledge.

79 House of Commons (2004) *Cars of the Future: Seventeenth Report of Session 2003–04 (HC 319-I).* House of Commons Transport Committee (pp. 1–54).

80 House of Commons (2004) *Cars of the Future: Seventeenth Report of Session 2003–04 (HC 319-I).* House of Commons Transport Committee (pp. 1–54).

81 B. Sharpe and T. Hodgson (2006) *Towards a Cyber-Urban Ecology*. Foresight Project on Intelligent Infrastructure Systems (p. 13).

82 D. Edgerton (2006) *The Shock of the Old: Technology and Global History since 1900*. London: Profile Books.

83 See C. Perrow (1999) *Normal Accidents*. Princeton: Princeton University Press.

Chapter 5 Organizations

1 See P. Hawken, A. Lovins and L. H. Lovins (2002) *Natural Capitalism: The Next Industrial Revolution*. London: Earthscan; and J. Motavalli (2000) *Forward Drive*. San Francisco: Sierra Club.

2 http://www.mobility.ch (accessed 22/11/07).

3 Car-sharing providers Zipcar and Flexcar have recently merged. The combined company will operate under the Zipcar brand and be headquartered in Cambridge, Massachusetts.

4 http://www.citycarclub.co.uk (accessed 17/01/08); http://www.streetcar.co.uk (accessed 17/01/08); http://www.whizzgo.co.uk (accessed 17/01/08).

5 Countryside-Agency (2004) *Rural Car Clubs*. The Countryside Agency – available online at http://www.carplus.org.uk/Resources/pdf/CA_report2004.pdf (accessed 24/07/06).

6 http://www.peasy.com/About-Us.aspx (accessed 02/07/07).

7 http://www.hitchsters.com (accessed 06/07/07).

8 See https://www.liftshare.org/uk/comstart.asp (accessed 10/04/08).

9 A. Karni (2007) 'Shared bicycles may be next on streets of New York', *The Sun*, New York: April 10, 2007 (accessed 14/07/07).

10 http://www.bicing.com – For English see: http://www.barcelona-on-line.es/noticies/noticia.asp?idIdioma=2&id Publicacio=1976 (accessed 22/07/07).

11 http://www.citizen-ecosystem.com/garden/2007/4/8/bicing-barcelona-sustainable-public-transportation.html (accessed 22/07/07).

12 J. Rifkin (2000) *The Age of Access*. London: Penguin.

13 See G. Vigar (2002) *The Politics of Mobility*. London: Spon.

14 Addison & Associates, L. Matson and C. Newson (2005) *Making Residential Travel Plans Work: Good Practice Guidelines for New Development*. London: Department for Transport.

15 See http://urbanhabitat.org/node/344 (accessed 19/03/08).

16 Transport-Innovator (2007) *Transport Innovator: January–February 2007*. The Bus Rapid Transit Policy Center.

17 For the UK, see Transport Direct, www.transportdirect.info (accessed 12/04/08).

18 WSP-Group (2003) *Vision 2030 – Final Report*. Highways Agency (p. 9).

19 The trial scheme, however, was suspended by Norwich Union in summer 2008.

20 S. Graham (2002) 'FlowCity: networked mobilities and the contemporary metropolis', *Journal of Urban Technology*, 9: 1–20; S. Graham (2004) 'Constructing premium network spaces: reflections on infrastructure networks and contemporary urban development', in R. Hanley (ed.) *Moving People, Goods, and Information in the 21st Century*. London: Routledge; S. Graham (2005) 'Software-sorted geographies'. *Progress in Human Geography*, 29: 562–580.

21 EU (2005) *Trans-European Transport Network: TEN-T Priority Axes and Projects 2005*. European Commission (pp. 1–73).

22 G. Gallopin, P. Raskin and R. Swart (1997) *Branch Points: Global Scenarios and Human Choice*. Stockholm

Environment Institute – Global Scenario Group (pp. 1–47).

23 R. Rogers (1997) *Cities for a Small Planet*. London: Faber and Faber (p. 38).

24 C. Benninger (2001) 'Principles of intelligent urbanism'. *Ekistics*, 69 (412), pp. 39–65.

25 Foresight (2006) *Intelligent Infrastructure Futures The Scenarios – Towards 2055*. Office of Science and Technology, Dept for Trade and Industry.

26 See J. Larsen, J. Urry and K. Axhausen (2006) *Mobilities, Networks, Geographies*. Aldershot: Ashgate; J. Urry (2007) *Mobilities*. Cambridge: Polity (chapter 11) on the enduring significance of 'meetings'.

27 See http://www.dft.gov.uk/pgr/sustainable/smarter-choices/ ctwwt/chapter12homeshopping (accessed 15/01/08).

28 M. Salzman and I. Matathia (2006) *Next. Now: Trends for the Future*. London: Palgrave Macmillan.

29 N. Gilman, D. Randall and P. Schwartz (2007) 'Impacts of climate change: a system vulnerability approach to consider the potential impacts to 2050 of a mid–upper greenhouse gas emissions scenario', *Global Business Network*, January 2007 (pp. 1–24).

30 Generally here, see G. Monbiot (2006) *Heat: How to Stop the Planet Burning*. London: Allen Lane (chapters 8, 9).

31 G. Monbiot (2006) *Heat: How to Stop the Planet Burning*. London: Allen Lane (p. 187).

32 See the various UK examples described in R. Willis, M. Webb and J. Wilsdon (2007) *The Disrupters. Lessons for Low-carbon Innovation from the New Wave of Environmental Pioneers*. London: Nesta.

33 R. Willis, M. Webb and J. Wilsdon (2007) *The Disrupters. Lessons for Low-carbon Innovation from the New Wave of Environmental Pioneers*. London: Nesta (p. 4).

34 K. Franz (2005) *Tinkering. Consumers Reinvent the Early Automobile*. Philadelphia: University of Pennsylvania Press.

35 E. von Hippel (2006) *Democratizing Innovation*. Cambridge, Massachusetts: MIT Press; and see N. Thrift (2008) *Non-Representational Theory*. London: Routledge, on 'Re-inventing invention' (chapter 2).

Chapter 6 Models

1 A. C. Clarke (2000) *Profiles of the Future* (2nd revised ed.). London: Indigo.

2 B. Mau (2004) *Massive Change*. London: Phaidon Press.

3 Cited in B. Mau (2004) *Massive Change*. London: Phaidon Press (p. 59).

4 R. Register (2006) *Ecocities: Rebuilding Cities in Balance with Nature*. British Columbia: New Society (p. 148).

5 M. Safdie (1997) *The City After the Automobile: An Architect's Vision*. New York: Basic Books (p. 166).

6 G. Monbiot (2006) *Heat*. London: Allen Lane (p. 169).

7 W. Siembab (2005) 'The smart sprawl strategy or how to avoid cannibalism in our cities' http://www.siembab.com/docs/smartsprawl.pdf (accessed 22/07/07).

8 J. H. Kunstler (2006) *The Long Emergency: Surviving the Converging Catastrophes of the 21ˢᵗ Century*. London: Atlantic Books (p. 248).

9 H. Girardet (2004) *Cities, People, Planet*. Chichester: Wiley-Academy (p. 141).

10 Foresight (2006) *Intelligent Infrastructure Futures The Scenarios – Towards 2055*. Office of Science and Technology, Dept for Trade and Industry.

11 Foresight (2006) *Intelligent Infrastructure Futures The Scenarios – Towards 2055*. Office of Science and Technology, Dept for Trade and Industry (p. 34).

12 A. Steffen (2005) 'Smart growth, smart places and bright green cities', http://www.worldchanging.com/archives/001920.html (accessed 27/07/07).

13 See http://www.bestpractices.org (accessed 27/07/07).

14 For a discussion on these practices, see H. Girardet (2004) *Cities, People, Planet*. Chichester: Wiley-Academy.

15 R. Pinderhughes (2004) *Alternative Urban Futures: Planning for Sustainable Development in Cities throughout the World*. New York: Rowman and Littlefield Publishers.

16 P. Newman (1999) 'Transport: reducing automobile dependence', in D. Satterthwaite (ed.) *The Earthscan Reader in Sustainable Cities*. London: Earthscan Publications Ltd.

17 H. Dittmar and G. Ohland (eds.) (2004) *The New Transit Town: Best Practices in Transit-Orientated Development*. Washington, DC: Island Press.

18 Available online at http://cnu.org/sites/files/charter_english.pdf (accessed 27/07/07).

19 See http://www.newurbanism.org/newurbanism.html (accessed 27/07/07).

20 See http://www.newurbanism.org/newurbanism.html (accessed 27/07/07).

21 See http://www.newurbanism.org/newurbanism.html (accessed 27/07/07).

22 See http://www.transitorienteddevelopment.org – italics in original (accessed 27/07/07).

23 See http://www.transitorienteddevelopment.org (accessed 27/07/07).

24 M. Glotz-Richter (2003) 'moving the city: a guided tour of the transport integration strategy in Bremen, Germany', http://www.communauto.com/images/03.coupures_de_presse/video_summary.pdf (accessed 17/07/07).

25 These figures are correct as of early 2007 and are expected to rise.

26 M. Glotz-Richter (2003) 'Moving the city: a guided tour of the transport integration strategy in Bremen, Germany', http://www.communauto.com/images/03. coupures_de_presse/video_summary.pdf   (accessed 17/07/07).

27 In partnership with Bill Dunster Architects and BioRegional Development Group, environmental consultants. See http://www.peabody.org.uk/pages/GetPage. aspx?id=179 (accessed 19/07/07).

28 See http://www.peabody.org.uk/pages/GetPage. aspx?id=179 (accessed 19/07/07).

29 See their homepage – http://transitiontowns.org (accessed 08/06/07).

30 See http://transitiontowns.org (accessed 08/06/07).

31 J. Ferry (2007) 'You are now entering an oil-free zone' *The Guardian*, April 19th.

32 See their homepage – http://transitiontowns.org (accessed 23/04/08).

33 See BBC (2007) 'China unveils climate change plan', http://news.bbc.co.uk/1/hi/world/asia-pacific/6717671. stm (accessed 04/06/07).

34 H. Girardet (2000) 'Cities, People, Planet'. Liverpool Schumacher Lectures in Urban Sustainability.

35 See also GreenBuildingPress (2007) 'Eco City design to be reviewed in Birmingham', http://www.newbuilder. co.uk/news/newsFullStory.asp?ID=1940   (accessed 25/06/07).

36 For more information visit the Worldwatch Institute – http://www.worldwatch.org.

37 See the Foster and Partners website on Masdar at http://www.fosterandpartners.com/Projects/1515/ Default.aspx (accessed 23/04/08).

38 J. Vidal (2008) 'Desert state channels oil wealth into world's first sustainable city', *The Guardian*, January 21st.

39 See the Foster and Partners website on Masdar at http:// www.fosterandpartners.com/Projects/1515/Default.aspx (accessed 23/04/08).

40 B. Mau (2004) *Massive Change*. London: Phaidon Press (p. 129).

41 For Linden Labs homepage see: http://lindenlab.com.

42 See press releases at http://lindenlab.com/pressroom/ releases/01_08_07 (accessed 28/04/08).

43 See 'What is Second Life', http://secondlife.com/whatis (accessed 28/04/08).

44 The current market value as of late April 2008 was L$265 = $1. See http://secondlife.com/whatis/economy-market. php (accessed 28/04/08).

45 For example, see: http://www.wired.com/gaming/virtu-alworlds/news/2006/02/70153 (accessed 28/04/08).

46 For example, see: http://money.cnn.com/2007/01/22/ magazines/fortune/secondlife_recruit.fortune; and http://www.aviationweek.com/aw/blogs/defense/index. jsp?plckController=Blog&plckScript=blogScript&plckE lementId=blogDest&plckBlogPage=BlogViewPost&plc kPostId=Blog%3a27ec4a53-dcc8-42d0-bd3a-01329aef-79a7Post%3acf3f0214-c16c-41b1-a0d8-53a7bc0e31ef; and http://news.bbc.co.uk/1/hi/technology/7274377.stm (accessed 28/04/08).

47 See homepage at http://www.virtualworlds2007.com (accessed 28/04/08).

Chapter 7 Scenarios

1 C. Abbott, P. Rogers and J. Sloboda (2007) *Beyond Terror. The Truth about the Real Threats to our World*. London: Rider.

2 See the analysis of climate denial in A. McCright and R. Dunlap (2000) 'Challenging global warming as a social problem: an analysis of the conservative movement's counter-claims', *Social Problems*, 49: 499–522.

3 B. Wisner et al. (2007) *Climate Change and Human Security*, http://www.radixonline.org/cchs.html (accessed 04/03/08).

4 T Homer-Dixon (1999) *Environment, Scarcity, and Violence*. Princeton: Princeton University Press; N. Stern (2007) *The Economics of Climate Change*. Cambridge: Cambridge University Press.

5 C. Abbott (2008) *An Uncertain Future: Law Enforcement, National Security and Climate Change*, Oxford Research Group, http://www.oxfordresearchgroup.org.uk/publications/briefing_papers/pdf/uncertainfuture.pdf (accessed 18/02/08).

6 C. Abbott (2008) *An Uncertain Future: Law Enforcement, National Security and Climate Change*, Oxford Research Group, http://www.oxfordresearchgroup.org.uk/publications/briefing_papers/pdf/uncertainfuture.pdf (accessed 18/02/08).

7 See Naomi Klein: 'Police state 2.0', *The Guardian*, June 3rd, 2008, G2 (pp. 4–9).

8 See http://www.mod.uk/DefenceInternet/DefenceNews/DefencePolicyAndBusiness/MetOfficeClimateChangeStudy CouldHelpIdentify FutureSecurityThreats.htm (accessed 20/02/08).

9 N. Gilman, D. Randall and P. Schwartz (2007) 'Impacts of climate change: a system vulnerability approach to consider the potential impacts to 2050 of a mid-upper greenhouse gas emissions scenario', *Global Business Network*, January (p. 12). And see Table 3.1 in N. Stern (2007) *The Economics of Climate Change*. Cambridge: Cambridge University Press,

which sets out the effects on water, food, health, land, environment and abrupt large-scale changes of varying levels of temperature increase.

10 C. Abbott (2008) *An Uncertain Future: Law Enforcement, National Security and Climate Change*, Oxford Research Group, http://www.oxfordresearchgroup.org.uk/publications/briefing_papers/pdf/uncertainfuture.pdf (accessed 18/02/08)

11 C. Abbott (2008) *An Uncertain Future: Law Enforcement, National Security and Climate Change*, Oxford Research Group, http://www.oxfordresearchgroup.org.uk/publications/briefing_papers/pdf/uncertainfuture.pdf (accessed 18/02/08) (p. 8).

12 C. Paskal (2007) 'How climate change is pushing the boundaries of security and foreign policy'. Chatham House, http://www.chathamhouse.org.uk/files/9250_bp0607 climatecp.pdf (accessed 04/03/08).

13 http://www.greencarcongress.com/2008/03/national-resear.html (accessed 29/03/08).

14 See *TimesOnline* – http://www.timesonline.co.uk/tol/news/world/asia/article2994650.ece (accessed 11/12/07).

15 M. Parry and others (2001) 'Millions at risk: defining critical climate change threats and targets', *Global Environmental Change*, 11: 81–3 (p. 81).

16 D. Pfeiffer (2006) *Eating Fossil Fuels*. Gabriola Island, BC: New Society Publishers.

17 The US Department of Agriculture claimed that in 2007 the country would use around 18–20 per cent of its total corn crop for ethanol production, increasing to 25 per cent by 2008. See B. Sauser (2007) 'Ethanol demand threatens food prices', *Technology Review*, Tuesday February 13th, http://www.technologyreview.com/read_article.aspx?ch=specialsections&sc=biofuels&id=18173&a= (accessed 12/11/07).

18 D. Pfeiffer (2006) *Eating Fossil Fuels*. Gabriola Island, BC: New Society Publishers (p. 2).

19 D. Pfeiffer (2006) *Eating Fossil Fuels*. Gabriola Island, BC: New Society Publishers (p. 25).

20 D. Pfeiffer (2006) *Eating Fossil Fuels*. Gabriola Island, BC: New Society Publishers (p. 24).

21 D. Pfeiffer (2006) *Eating Fossil Fuels*. Gabriola Island, BC: New Society Publishers (p. 83).

22 See D. Harvey (2005) *A Brief History of Neo-Liberalism*. Oxford: Oxford University Press; N. Klein (2007) *The Shock Doctrine*. London: Penguin Allen Lane. Klein (p. 166) notes that Chicago School alumni included by 1999 twenty-five Government Ministers and more than a dozen central bank presidents!

23 N. Klein (2007) *The Shock Doctrine*. London: Penguin Allen Lane (pp. 3–21).

24 D. Harvey (2005) *A Brief History of Neo-Liberalism*. Oxford: Oxford University Press (pp. 159–61).

25 D. Harvey (2005) *A Brief History of Neo-Liberalism*. Oxford: Oxford University Press (p. 3).

26 N. Stern (2006) *Stern Review: The Economics of Climate Change*. London: House of Commons, 27 pages (p. 1).

27 J. M. Keynes (1961) *The General, Theory of Employment, Interest and Money*. London: Macmillan (orig. 1936) (p. 383).

28 N. Stern (2007) *The Economics of Climate Change*. Cambridge: Cambridge University Press (p. 644).

29 This is best explained in D. Harvey (2005) *The New Imperialism*. Oxford: Oxford University Press.

30 See D. Harvey (2005) *The New Imperialism*. Oxford: Oxford University Press. On Europe, see J. Rifkin (2004) *The European Dream*. New York: Penguin Putnam.

31 J. Rifkin (2004) *The European Dream*. New York: Penguin Putnam (p. 14).

32 B. Adam and C. Groves (2007) *Future Matters. Action, Knowledge, Ethics*. Leiden: Brill. See J. Urry (2008) 'Climate change, travel and complex futures', *British Journal of Sociology*, 59: 261–79.

33 See R. Hickman and D. Banister (2006) *Towards a 60% Reduction in UK Transport Carbon Dioxide Emissions: A Scenario Building and Backcasting Approach*. London: University College, London. http://www.vibat.org/publications/pdf/eceee_paper.pdf (accessed 31/03/08). See especially p. 5 where it is suggested that Amory Lovins, whose innovations we discussed in chapter 4, invented the method of backcasting.

34 N. N. Taleb (2007) *The Black Swan*. London: Penguin (p. 173).

35 See Foresight (2006) *Intelligent Infrastructure Futures The Scenarios – Towards 2055*. London: Office of Science and Technology, Dept for Trade and Industry. John Urry was involved in this scenario building coordinated by the Henley Centre and Waverley Consultants. Sixty 'drivers' of change were examined. For another scenario building exercise, see K. Anderson and others (2006) *Decarbonising Modern Societies: Integrated Scenario Process and Workshops*. London and Manchester: Tyndall Centre.

36 J. Timmons Roberts and B. Parks (2007) *A Climate of Injustice*. Cambridge, Massachusetts: MIT Press.

37 G. H Gallopin, P. Raskin and R. Swart (1997) *Branch Points: Global Scenarios and Human Choice*. Stockholm: Stockholm Environment Institute – Global Scenario Group (pp. 35–6).

38 A recent suggestion on rebuilding market towns in the UK captures something of this future; each town would have some special characteristic in order to attract and to keep residents there and not travelling elsewhere.

39 D. Harvey (2000) *Spaces of Hope*. Edinburgh: Edinburgh University Press.

40 See the classic N. Klein (2000) *No Logo*. London: Flamingo.

41 J. Kunstler (2006) *The Long Emergency: Surviving the Converging Catastrophes of the 21st Century*. London: Atlantic Books.

42 J. Kunstler (2006) *The Long Emergency: Surviving the Converging Catastrophes of the 21st Century*. London: Atlantic Books (p. 270).

43 D. Harvey (2000) *Spaces of Hope*. Edinburgh: Edinburgh University Press (pp. 270–1).

44 Foresight (2006) *Intelligent Infrastructure Futures The Scenarios – Towards 2055*. Office of Science and Technology, Dept for Trade and Industry.

45 G. Gallopin, P. Raskin and R. Swart (1997) *Branch Points: Global Scenarios and Human Choice*. Stockholm: Stockholm Environment Institute – Global Scenario Group (p. 29).

46 G. Gallopin, P. Raskin, R. Swart (1997) *Branch Points: Global Scenarios and Human Choice*. Stockholm: Stockholm Environment Institute – Global Scenario Group (p. 34).

47 See J. Tainter (1988) *The Collapse of Complex Societies*. New York: Cambridge University Press; R. Woodbridge (2004) *The Next World War: Tribes, Cities, Nations, and Ecological Decline*. Toronto: University of Toronto Press.

48 J. Mouawad (2008) 'The construction site called Saudi Arabia', *The New York Times*, January 20th, 2008, http://www.nytimes.com/2008/01/20/business/world-business/20saudi.html (accessed 29/01/08).

49 As argued in K. Hannam, M. Sheller and J. Urry (2006) 'Editorial: Mobilities, Immobilities and Moorings', *Mobilities*, 1: 1–22.

50 J. Timmons Roberts and B. Parks (2007) *A Climate of Injustice*. Cambridge, Massachusetts: MIT Press.

51 This depicts the future through a bleak, dystopian, impoverished society facing a breakdown of civil order resulting from oil shortages.

52 N. Klein (2007) *The Shock Doctrine*. London: Penguin Allen Lane (p. 21).

53 Foresight (2006) *Intelligent Infrastructure Futures The Scenarios – Towards 2055*. Office of Science and Technology, Dept for Trade and Industry.

54 P. Peters (2006) *Time, Innovation and Mobilities*. London: Routledge (p. 132).

55 J. Tiffin and C. Kissling (2007) *Transport Communications*. London: Kegan Paul (p. 204).

56 On rationing air miles, see G. Monbiot (2006) *Heat. How to Stop the Planet Burning*. London: Allen Lane (p. 173).

57 For details, see B. Sharpe and T. Hodgson (2006) *Towards a Cyber-Urban Ecology*. Foresight Project on Intelligent Infrastructure Systems (pp. 1–44). See Foresight (2006) *Trends and Drivers in Intelligent Infrastructure Systems A Literature Review for the Foresight Project on Intelligent Infrastructure Systems*. Foresight Project on Intelligent Infrastructure Systems.

58 E. Beinhocker (2006) *The Origin of Wealth*. London: Random House (pp. 333, 374).

59 See Information Commissioner (2006) A *Report on the Surveillance Society*. London: The Surveillance Network; S. Graham (2005) 'Software-sorted geographies', *Progress in Human Geography*, 29: 562–80. For general information see the journal *Surveillance and Society* – http://www.surveillance-and-society.org/index.htm (accessed 05/11/06).

60 Information Commissioner (2006) *A Report on the Surveillance Society*. London: The Surveillance Network. See also BBC report – http://news.bbc.co.uk/1/hi/uk/6108496.stm (accessed 05/11/06). There are up to 5 million CCTV cameras in Britain – about one for every

12 people – more than any other society, although China would seem to be catching up fast. For a recent dramatic examination of the politics of contemporary surveillance, see the 2008 BBC drama *The Last Enemy* – http://www. bbc.co.uk/drama/lastenemy (accessed 04/04/08).

61 See the essays in D. Miller (ed.) (2000) *Car Cultures*. Oxford: Berg.

62 E. Burke (1790) *Reflections on the Revolution in France*. New York: Bartleby (pp. 143–4). See N. Stern (2007) *The Economics of Climate Change*. Cambridge: Cambridge University Press (chapter 2A).

63 The Metropolitan Police in London have recently been allowed access to congestion charging photo evidence so that they can track the movement of cars suspected of terrorist offences; see http://news.bbc.co.uk/1/hi/uk_politics/6902543.stm (accessed 20/07/07).

INDEX